Tearing Walls of Fear

The Role of Education in the Outbreak of the Arab Spring Uprisings

Mohamed El Bouchikhi

SUN MOON CENTER FOR ISLAMIC STUDIES
SUN MOON UNIVERSITY

Tearing Walls of Fear The Role of Education in the Outbreak of the Arab Spring Uprisings

First edition printing: August 25, 2015
First edition publishing: August 28, 2015

Writer / Mohamed El Bouchikhi
Published by Sun Moon University Press (Hwang, Sun Jo)
Registration no. / No. 9
Date of Registration / September 25, 1998
Address / (31460) 221 Sunmoon-ro, Tangjeong-myeon, Asan-si, Chungnam-do, Republic of Korea
Telephone no. / +81-41-530-2827 Fax no. / +82-41-530-2979

Printed at Dahae (+82-22266-9247)

* This book was originally for my PhD dissertation:
The Arab Spring: The Role of Education in The Outbreak of The Prodemocracy Movements in The Arab World in 2011

Price KRW 12,000

ISBN 978-89-8423-786-5 93340

"Those Who Steadfastly Persevere Will Receive Their Recompense Generously Without Limits"

Contents

• Chapter I •

Introduction

By early 1960s, when most of the Arab countries were newly independent, democracy was not a hot issue,[1] rather, building the new nation, educating people, and nationalizing all aspects of life were of a primary concern for the newly independent nations. As the time went by, the region[2] was in a slippery slope into diversified forms

[1] Ibrahim Elbadawi and Samir Makdessi, "Introduction," Ibrahim Elbadawi and Samir Makdessi (eds.), *Democracy in the Arab World: Explaining the Deficit* (New York: Routledge, 2011), p. 1.

[2] This study borrows the term 'Arab region' instead of 'Middle East and North Africa (MENA), because the latter contains non-Arab countries such

of tyranny. While the world has undergone significant transitions and democratization efforts with varying degrees of success, the Arab region remained 'exception' for the analogy and stuck to authoritarianism.

In mid-December 2010, a small event in the smallest Arab country in North Africa, Tunisia occurred to reshape the whole region and the fate of millions of Arabs. When Mohamed Bouazizi set himself on fire as a protest against bribe-seeking policewoman's harassment, nobody would have guessed that this event would spark "The Arab Spring."[3] The Arab Spring can be defined as a set of popular uprisings that galvanized millions of Arabs to the streets from Casablanca to Damascus. It started with the Jasmine Revolution in Tunisia, which had contagiously triggered spontaneous and simultaneous massive demonstrations. By mid-February 2011, millions of people were taking to the streets in Egypt, Yemen, Bahrain, Libya,

---

as Malta, Iran, Israel, and Turkey. The Arab region is defined according to two criteria, the language criteria, and the membership to Arab League.

[3] Marc Lynch, "Obama's 'Arab Spring'?" http://mideast.foreignpolicy.com/posts/2011/01/06/obamas_arab_spring. (Search date: November 7, 2012)

and Morocco, and by mid-March, Syria was a full member of the Arab Spring club.

The Jasmine Revolution played an imminent role in tearing walls of fear and encouraged people to raise their voices for freedom and call for change. Thousands of Tunisians flooded the streets chanting *the people want to overthrow the regime*, forcing Ben Ali, the 23 years iron fist-ruling president, to flee the country in January 14, 2011.[4] During 18 days of heavy peaceful demonstrations, Mubarak, the 30 years iron-fist ruling president, was forced to step down, arrested and driven to justice. He was the first Arab leader to be ousted and jailed by his own people. In Yemen, youth-driven peaceful demonstrations were diverted to a tribal conflict and drove the country to the verge of a civil war. The long-standing rule of Saleh came to an end as he stepped down in November 23, 2011. In Bahrain young activists launched their first wave of demonstrations on the 'day of rage' in February 14, 2011. A Saudi military intervention

---

[4] Kenneth Chamberlain, "TIMELINE: Revolt in the Middle East and North Africa," http://www.nationaljournal.com/timeline-revolt-in-the-middle-east-and-north-africa-20110128. (Search date: November 7, 2012)

in March 15, aborted a blooming revolution, only few miles away from the house of Saud. In Libya, as riots broke out in Banghazi, in February 15, 2011, Qaddafi vowed, in a long televised speech, to crack down the rebellions. As Libya went under a civil war, NATO launched its air strikes ended up by killing Gaddafi in October 20.

In Jordan and Morocco, peaceful demonstrations demanded freedom and political reform and both kings replied with political reforms and successfully absorbed the mass rage. In March 15, 2011, the uprising broke out in Syria and the country quickly slipped into chaos. Algerians rampaged through the streets as their government raised the prices of key goods, but they failed in galvanizing mass population to the streets like other Arab Spring countries. In Oman, protestors focused their attention on the rising prices of basic goods and on corruption but their main demand was political reform.

To what extent did education contribute to the outbreak of the Arab spring uprisings early 2011? This question is relevant to understand the causes and circumstances that led to the sudden eruption of the Arab

Spring uprisings as well as the region's long-standing immunity to democracy.

The Arab Spring uprisings are the result of a process of modernization and developments that the Arab people went through, characterized by the rise of a new Arab public sphere. During 2000s, the Arab region witnessed the rise of young generation that spent their formative years in the virtual world planning for their future moves. They benefitted from the new technology to engage themselves in valiant arguments, debates, and discussions about the common issues. The Arab youth grew with new hopes of change using their own capabilities to make it real, and when Bouazizi's act of desperation initiated the region's cascade of events, they were ready to take to the streets.[5]

---

[5] Marc Lynch, *The Arab Uprising: The Unfinished Revolutions of The New Middle East* (New York: Public Affairs, 2012), p. 15.

* GMEI was "part of President Bush's, by which the expansion of political rights and political participation in the Muslim world is meant to combat the appeal of Islamist extremism." Tamara Cofman. Wittes, "The New U.S. Proposal for a Greater Middle East Initiative: An Evaluation forward strategy of freedom" http://www.brookings.edu/research/papers/2004/05/10middleeast-wittes (Search Date: July 3, 2015)

A shift in the American policy in the region took place with the American invasion of Iraq in 2003, when G.W. Bush claimed the compatibility of Islam with democracy, and the importance of initiating democratization process. In 2004, Bush administration launched the 'Greater Middle East Initiative' (GMEI) to democratize the Muslim area from North Africa to Central Asia*. Since then, trainings were offered to young activists from Arab countries, to prepare them to peacefully mobilize mass population using social media to change the regimes. This shift in the American policy is due to the emergence of new international actors, namely Russia and China, which will challenge the American dominance of the region.[6]

The Arab Spring was a reflection that the Arab region has reached a peak of a combined political tyranny with socio-economic marginalization, and high inequalities. This was associated with high levels of corruption and centralization of economic resources under the control of few that were either part of the ruling families or their

---

[6] Tarik Ramadan, *L'Islam Et Le Réveil Arabe* (Paris: Presses du Châtelet, 2011), p. 28.

inner circles. The spread of corruption and lack of accountability reached levels that could not be ignored or unfelt by the citizens.

The role of education was crucial in the rise of a new Arab public sphere, because using Internet tools and understanding TV programs, mainly Al-Jazeera, requires a certain level of education. Educational attainment is an important element in the creation of the Arab public sphere itself. The sudden outbreak of the Jasmine Revolution and the quick collapse of the Tunisian regime surprised Western powers, which had always provided support to the tyrant regimes. They were aware that Islamists would be the most benefiters from democracy. The 1992 elections in Algeria and 2006 in Palestine showed vivid examples of how Islamists devastated the political scene through democratic elections. Although the socio-economic factors played an undeniable role in triggering the uprisings, the Arab region witnessed an economic downturn since 1980s, when World Bank provided loans and engaged these countries into adjustment structural policies. Poverty levels have risen among the population and inequalities were widened between the poor majority and rich minority. Arab countries also witnessed many failed uprisings for the past 30 years; meanwhile the 2011 were successful in overthrowing many leaders. These successful uprisings coincided with unprecedented levels of education that the region has reached.

It is important to note that this essay does not downplay the importance of the previous analyses, nor it claims to provide the most complete and accurate analysis of the causes of the Arab uprisings. Rather, as the narrowed-down question implies this essay seeks to identify only the extent to which the spread of education analysis can explain the main puzzle of this research. The rationale for raising this question is to further explore on the initial observation that the spread of education among youth has an impact on providing a fertile environment for democracy. It is important also to mention that the aim of this essay is to emphasize the contribution of education in the outbreak of the Arab Spring uprisings, regardless if they succeeded or failed in establishing democratic regimes.

The Arab World has entered a new era where the widespread of education has reshaped people's minds and made the area ready for change. A combination of people's awareness, resulted from the spread of education mainly among youth sparked the uprisings, and the rising rates of unemployment among educated youth, mainly university graduates, fueled and assured the spread and the continuity of the uprisings.

The formidable results of spreading education have embarked the Arab region on a cultural and mental era, which facilitates the road towards democracy. Education is a powerful tool in bringing changes in men, acculturating individuals, developing, and universalizing their minds. Thus, the Arab Spring is a set of popular uprisings driven by educated youth combining education and democracy. Arguing education as prerequisite for democracy goes back to the writings of John Dewey on the relation between education and democracy. He set an entire philosophy of democratic government, which saw the basic requirement for democracy in the spread of education.[7]

Education is argued to promote democracy both because it enables developing a culture of democracy, and because it leads to greater prosperity that is thought to cause political development. This essay borrows the form of the modernized theory popularized by Lipset, which emphasizes the role of education as well as economic growth in promoting political development in general and democracy in particular. Education is argued to be a prerequisite for democracy, because it "presumably broadens men's outlooks, enables them to understand the need for norms of tolerance, restrains them from adhering to extremist and monistic doctrines, and increases their capacity to make rational electoral choices."[8] Moreover, "if we cannot say that a 'high' level of education is a sufficient condition for democracy, the available evidence does suggest that it comes close to being a necessary

---

[7] John Dewey, *Democracy and Education: An Introduction To The Philosophy of Education* (New York: Macmillan Company, 1916).

[8] Seymour Martin Lipset, "Some Social Requisites of Democracy: Economic Development and Political Legitimacy," *The American Political Review*, Vol. 53, No. 1 (1959), p. 79.

condition."[9] A common view clearly articulated by the modernization theory claims that "high levels of schooling are both a prerequisite for democracy and a major cause of democratization."[10]

Literacy, and education more generally, are of primary importance for democracy. But literacy seems to be more important as a foundation for democracy than any other aspect of modernization.[11] The role of education goes beyond enabling men to read and understand the news, or providing a political literacy to comprehend the issues of politics to be effective political leaders; it helps to break down traditionalism, and to develop new attitudes and values.[12] It is argued that the higher education achieved the more likely to believe in democratic values and support democratic practices. A better-educated population of a

---

9 Seymour M. Lipset, *op. cit.* p. 80.

10 Daron Acemoglu, Simon Johnson, James A. Robinson, and Pierre Yared, "From Education to Democracy?" *The American Economic Review*, Vol. 95, No. 2 (May 2005), p. 49.

11 James Roland Pennock, *Democratic Political Theory* (Princeton: Princeton University Press, August 1979), p. 59.

12 Alex Inkeles, "Making Modern Men, On the Causes and Consequences of Industrial Change in Six Developing Countries," *American Journal of Sociology*, Vol. 75, No. 2 (1969), p. 216.

country provides better chances for democracy to grow and sustain. The spread of education in Germany is linked to rejecting dictatorship in post Nazi era.[13] The evidence on the contribution of education to democracy is more direct and strong in connection with individual behavior within countries.

The spread of education has contributed to the emergence of a young educated generation who successfully mobilized mass population early 2011. Unprecedented levels of education had been reached in post-independence era, and widely spread among the population. People's awareness combined with the rising rates of unemployment among educated youth mainly university graduates fueled the uprisings, unlike the *bread uprisings* of 1980s. An educated generation sparked the uprisings using Internet and social media to mobilize mass population; while unemployed university graduates fueled the demonstrations through the Arab streets to end up with the Arab Spring.

In order to answer the main question, we will compare the spread of education in Arab Spring and non-Arab

---

[13] James Roland Pennock (1979), *op. cit.*, p. 60.

spring countries, and we will explore the contribution of education in the outbreak of the Arab uprisings. The dependent variable is the outbreak of the Arab Spring uprisings, and the independent variable is the spread education. In measuring the independent variable, this essay looks to the contribution of the spread of education mainly among youth through four education indicators: public spending, gross enrollment rates, literacy rates, and gender parity in education. This essay uses method of comparative case study to explore the contribution of education in the outbreak of the Arab Spring uprisings early 2011. As Lijphart has pointed out, comparative method is "resorted when the number of cases available for analysis is so small,"[14] and although the number of cases compared in this essay is small, but subjecting them to intensive comparative analysis would be more promising than a more cursory statistical analysis of many cases.

The comparative cases will be Bahrain and Sudan, which were carefully selected, both countries share

---

[14] Arend Lijphart, "Comparative Politics and the Comparative Method," *The American Political Science Review*, Vol. 65, No. 3 (September 1971), p. 684.

relatively similar conditions that might ignite an uprising, from being under stale regimes to being fully resourced countries with an apparent lack of social justice. The main difference remains educational profile of both countries, while Bahrain has the highest among the Arab countries, Sudan's profile is very low. The period that is covered by this essay is the last 25 years, since the average age of the young educated people who drove these uprisings through the Arab streets is around 25 years. We will cover the Arab countries that went under the Arab Spring demonstrations early 2011; even they were hit with different intensity.

This essay is organized into five chapters. Following the Introduction, chapter II will explore the Arab region in the eve of the outbreak of the Arab Spring uprisings, by shedding the light on the youth bulge as catalyst of change, the spread of education, the common characteristics, and a chronology of the uprisings. Chapter III will explore the relation between the Arab Spring and Education. Chapter IV compares the cases of Bahrain and Sudan as the main comparative cases with regard to the spread of education through four education indicators.

These indicators are public spending on education, literacy rates, gross enrollment rates, and gender parity in education. This chapter will explain why these indicators were chosen to measure the spread of education.

The last chapter summarizes that the spread of education makes a plausible explanatory factor that accounts for the causes of the Arab Spring in Bahrain and its absence in Sudan. This chapter will give some questions based on the findings of this study for further research on the democratization issue in the Arab region.

Chapter II

The Eve of The Uprisings

For decades, the Arab region stood as the largest area in the world to remain immune to democracy, while the third wave of democratization was only a few miles away from the Arab borders. Suddenly spontaneous, simultaneous, and unexpected waves of young people flooded to the Arab streets from Rabat to Damascus. They forced the Tunisian president to flee the country in four weeks and the Egyptian president to step down in three weeks of massive demonstrations. Waves of raged people took arms and killed Qaddafi in a six-month-bloody militarized revolution; they also obliged Ali Abdullah

Saleh, who miraculously escaped death, to leave his palace, and launched a peaceful, later a militarized, revolution against Al-Assad regime. Enraged waves have also seriously challenged the monarchies of Morocco, Bahrain, Oman, and Jordan.

The Arab Spring is a set of youth-driven popular uprisings, which shed the light on the region's 100 million strong youth population, and its critical role in reshaping the political, economic, and social structures in the Arab world. Youth under the age of 25 – as the fastest growing segment of the populations – represent an estimated and amazing 60% of the region's population. In most of the Arab countries, approximately 30% of the population is between the ages of 15 and 29, making it one of the most youthful regions in the world. [15] This youth bulge coincided with high levels of education. The region has generously spent on education more than East Asia and Latin America. This environment made the region fertile for revolution and ready to take action. The Arab Spring

---

15 "Challenges to Human Security in the Arab Countries," http://www.arab-hdr.org/publications/other/ahdr/ahdr2009e.pdf. (Search date: November 15, 2012)

prodemocracy movements share some common characteristics. They are leaderless, educated-youth driven, non-ideological, and nonviolent movements where women and the usage of the Internet and social media played a pivotal role in mobilizing the mass population to take to the streets.

2.1. The Arab Region

The Arab region is diversified demographically, geographically, politically, and socio-economically. In terms of demography, as indicated in Table 2.1, the region contains countries with large population like of Egypt with 84,474 million, and countries with small population like Bahrain of 807,000 people. North Africa is the most populous region among the Arab world with 168,198 million; Egypt makes half of it and Libya is the smallest with 6,546 million. In West Asian Arab countries (Levant & Iraq), the total population is 69,108 million, led by Iraq 31,467 million; meanwhile the total population of Arabian Peninsula has reached 63,480 million, which ranges from

26 million in both Saudi and Yemen to 807,000 in Bahrain. In Sub-Saharan Arab countries, the total population is 57,487 million, led by Sudan pre-secession with 43 million.

Geographically, the Region is characterized by extreme differences in land. For example, Sudan (pre-secession), as the largest country in the region with 2.5 million square kilometers, is the tenth largest country in the world. In contrast, the region's smallest country, Bahrain, covers just 750 square kilometers. Socio-economically, perhaps no other region in the world is marked by such extreme disparities in wealth as the Arab region. Three countries (Comoros, Djibouti, and Somalia) are classified as the least developed by the United Nations and are among the poorest countries in the world. At the other end of the spectrum Kuwait, Qatar, and the United Arab Emirates are among the world's wealthiest nations, as reflected in their per capita Gross Domestic Product.[16]

Arab region – defined here as the Middle East and North Africa (MENA)- is home to five major and distinct

---

[16] Barry Mirkin, "Population Levels: Trends and Policies in the Arab Region: Challenges and Opportunities," http://www.arab-hdr.org/publications/other/ahdrps/paper01-en.pdf. (Search date: November 12, 2012)

ethnical groups: Turks, Persians, Kurds, Arabs, and Berbers. There are numerous sub-divisions and tribes within these four categories. Religion is a significant factor for the people of Arab region, which many people in the region identify themselves with their religion before any other characteristic. "The area is well-known for being home to a vast Muslim population, but the area is also home to numerous religious minorities, namely Christians and Jews, but also smaller religious groups, such as the Druze, Maronites, and Alawites. These religious minorities were not subject to Islamic laws related to personal matters under the Ottomans; these groups were permitted to use their own religion as basis for determining rules for divorce, marriage, and other family matters."[17]

Since the independence, Arab political regimes have generally been characterized by varying forms of authoritarian rule, such autocratic monarchies in Saudi

---

[17] Krysten Young, "Democratization in the Middle East and North Africa: Challenges Explanations and Suggestions for the Future," http://web3.unt.edu/honors/eaglefeather/wp-content/2011/08/Young-Krysten-081711-Final.pdf. (Search date: November 13, 2012)

Arabia, single party regimes as the cases of Iraq and Syria Baath party, military regimes, where most of Arab regimes came to power though coups and shifted to civil regimes and adopted single party such as the case of Sudan. They personalized the state, and shared its institutions among their relatives and their inner close circles. Moreover, they introduced a new concept: jumlukiya (*repubmonarchy* or *monarpublicanism*)[18], which indicates the situation where the presidents in republic regimes handover the power to their family members, mainly sons. In the post-Cold War world, it was introduced first by North Korea in 1994, and then Syria in 2000. Other regimes in Tunisia, Egypt, Yemen, Libya, and Algeria, were preparing to place their relatives on the head of their states, but the outbreak of the Arab Spring halted the process.

What characterized the Arab region was its immunity to democracy while the whole world was witnessing a global trend towards democratization. The persistency of autocracy and the lack of intentions to democratize with

---

[18] Juan Cole, "Saad's Revolution," http://www.truthdig.com/report/item/saads_revolution_20110131 (Search date: Sep 19, 2012)

the full support from foreign powers was the direct cause of the fatal rise of religious fundamentalism in the area. The blind support given in return to protect these powers' interests of full access to oil resources. The denial of domestic demands for sharing power, freedom, and social justice made the region a fertile land for fundamentalism to grow and become an imminent global menace.[19]

After the collapse of the Soviet Union in 1991, under his new world order's four-point plan, George Bush promised spreading democracy in the Arab world, and exercised pressure on Arab regimes to show some intention towards democracy. When Francis Fukuyama suggests that human history should be viewed in terms of a battle of ideologies, where liberalism was the winner, the Arab region witnessed seemingly promising beginnings of reform with the rise of Liberalism, but there was no substantial changes[20]. Aborting the democratic process in Algeria as the Islamic Salvation Front swept

---

[19] Fareed Zakaria, "The Politics of Rage: Why Do They Hate Us?" http://www.thedailybeast.com/newsweek/2001/10/14/the-politics-of-rage-why-do-they-hate-us.htm. (Search date: Nov 15, 2012)

[20] Peter Mansfield, *A History of The Middle East*, Nicolas Pelham (Revis. and Upd.) (Penguin Books 2013), P. 382.

the first round of 1991 elections alarmed the Arab regime to distance themselves from democracy, and convinced Islamists to pursue other ways than democracy, which opened the doors to a fatale era of violence. Several Arab countries suffered from a systematic rise of radical ideologies and violent movements that had their root causes in state repression and economic deprivation.[21]

Table 2.1: Total Population and Average Annual Rate of Change, 1970-205

Country	Total population (thousands)			Average annual rate of population change (percentage)		
	1970	2010	2050	1970-1975	2005-2010	2045-2050
Arab region	127,865	359,273	598,174	2,8	2,1	0,8
Algeria	13,745	35,423	49,610	3,1	1,5	0,4
Bahrain	220	807	1,277	4,3	2,1	0,6
Comoros	238	691	1,226	2,6	2,3	0,9
Djibouti	162	879	1,469	6,5	1,8	0,9
Egypt	35,575	84,474	129,533	2,1	1,8	6,6
Iraq	10,210	31,467	63,995	3,3	2,2	1,1
Jordan	1,623	6,472	10,241	3,5	3,0	0,7
Kuwait	744	3,051	5,240	6,0	2,4	0,8
Lebanon	2,443	4,255	5,033	2,3	0,8	0,0
Libya	1,994	6,546	9,819	4,3	2,0	0,6
Mauritania	1,149	3,366	6,061	2,8	2,4	1,0
Morocco	15,310	31,381	42,583	2,5	1,2	0,3

21 Amr Hamzawy, "Understanding Arab Political Reality: One Lens Is Not Enough," http://www.carnegieendowment.org/files/PO15.hamzawy.FINAL.pdf. (Search date: Sep 17, 2012)

Palestine	1,096	4,409	10,265	2,7	3,2	1,4
Oman	747	2,905	4,878	4,1	2,1	0,7
Qatar	111	1,508	2,316	8,6	10,7	0,7
Saudi Arabia	5,745	26,246	43,658	4,7	2,1	0,7
Somalia	3,600	9,359	23,522	2,7	2,3	1,7
Sudan	15,039	43,192	75,884	3,0	2,2	0,9
Syria	6,371	22,505	36,911	3,4	3,3	0,8
Tunisia	5,127	10,374	12,711	2,0	1,0	0,1
UAE	225	4,707	8,253	17,2	2,8	1,0
Yemen	6,391	24,256	53,689	2,1	2,9	1,3

Sources: World Bank Central Database and UNESCO Institute for Statistics Statistical Yearbooks 2011

2.2. Youth Bulge in the Arab World

Youth bulge refers to a cohort of youth between the age of 15 and 25 that is usually large relative to the adult population in a society. Historically, it has been associated with times of political turmoil, and often plays an outstanding role in political violence. The literature on youth bulges has focused in particular on spontaneous and low-intensity unrest, such as nonviolent protests, riots, and rebellions.[22] Countries that witness youth bulge

[22] Henrik Urdal, "The Demographics of Political Violence: Youth Bulges, Security, and Conflicts," Lael Brainard and Derek Chollet (eds.), *Too Poor for*

are more likely to attain stable liberal democracy than countries with more mature age structure.[23]

"Historical research has linked youth bulges to revolutions in 17th century England, 18th century France, 20th century Indonesia (Goldstone 2002, Moller 1968); to political activism in Western and Middle Eastern countries (Huntington 96); to the presence of warfare throughout the world (Mesquida and Winner 1999, Urdal 2002)."[24] As the Arab region continues to fascinate and concern the rest of the world with two thirds of all known petroleum reserves, its population size outweighs its economic and political importance. It has the world's

---

Peace? Global Poverty, Conflict, and Security in the 21st Century (Washington D.C: Brookings Institution, 2007), p. 90.

[23] Richard P. Cincota, "Half A Change: Youth Bulges And Transition To Liberal Democracy," http://www.wilsoncenter.org/sites/default/files/Report13_ Cincotta.pdf. (Search date: September 2, 2012)

[24] Daniel Hart, Robert Atkins, Patrick Markey, and James Youniss, "Youth Bulges In Communities: The Effect of Age Structure on Adolescent Civic Knowledge and Civic Participation," *Psychological Science*, Vol. 15, No. 9 (2004), p. 591.

second fastest growing population after sub-Saharan Africa.[25]

During the last three decades, Arab region witnessed a notable decline of the fertility rates, which had dropped from 6.8 children per woman in 1975 to 3.5 in 2005. After the demographic transition, the levels of fertility rates in Arab countries are almost as low as in the Western world. Lebanon and Tunisia dropped down to 1.7 and 2.0 children per woman, respectively. Some countries are on the right track like Morocco 2.4, Algeria 2.6 and to some extent Libya 2.9 children per woman. Meanwhile, others have not fallen yet below 3 children, like Egypt, Syria, Jordan, Iraq, Saudi Arabia, and United Arab Emirates, but Yemen, with 6.2 children per woman remains the country with the highest fertility rate in the Arab world.[26] In general, the population in the Arab world is young, much

---

[25] Farzaneh Roudi Fahimi and Mary Mederios Kent, "Challenges and Opportunities: The Population of Middle East and North Africa," *Population Bulletin*, Vol. 62, No. 2 (2007), p. 3.

[26] Youssef Courbage and Emmnuel Todd, *A Convergence of Civilizations: The Transformation of Muslim Societies*, George Holoch (trans.) (New York: Columbia University Press 2011), p. 46.

below the world average of 2.8.[27] Due to the rapid declining death and slow declining fertility rates, Arab population's size witnessed a significant increase since 1970, and it is expected to increase in the coming five decades. Iraq, Yemen, and the Palestine will continue to see a rapid growth over the coming years, as shown in Table 2.1. Over the coming decade, approximately 65% of the population of the region will be less than 24 years old.

Currently more than 100 million people between the ages of 15 and 29 live in the Arab world, making up to 30 % of the region's population and almost 47% of the working age population. In some societies, this trend of large youth cohorts will persist for another 40 years. Mohamed Bouazizi was one of the more than 100 million 15 to 29 year-olds living in the Arab region today and making up the youth bulge in the region's demographic profile. Some states with high proportions of young people below

---

27 Antonello Cabras, "The Implications of The Youth bulge in MENA Populations," http://www.nato-pa.int/Default.asp?SHORTCUT=2342. (Search date: November 12, 2012)

the age of 24 include: Yemen at 65.3%, Saudi Arabia at 62.3%, Iraq at 61.7%, Iran at 59.3%, and Algeria at 56.5%.[28]

The population growth is associated with spread of education, rapid growth of the Internet access, unlimited broadcasting channels, social media, and instant communication, which are quickly changing the lives and minds of youth, and widening the generation gap between young people and their parents and decision-makers.

2.3. Significant Efforts in Spreading Education

Education is a powerful force that can speed up economic growth, improve income distribution, facilitate social mobility, and reduce poverty. It can also improve the quality of life for citizens by contributing to longer life expectancy, lower fertility and infant mortality rates, and a more cohesive national identity. The pursuit of education is among the foundations of positive social,

---

[28] Patrick Wrigly, "Youth Bulges in The Middle East and North Africa: Risk or Assets?" http://cmimarseille.org/_src/SELM4_WBFastBrief74.pdf. (Search date: January 12, 2012)

economic and political transformations in any society. In a modern rapidly changing world, societies aspire to provide rising generations with the necessary knowledge to deal with present and future challenges, ingraining national responsibility to achieve such in the minds of the public. Education is the most critical investment of any society in its population, because of its crucial impacts on the society itself and as well as on the people.[29]

In the aftermath of the region's independence, education was very low and mainly spread among men in urbanized areas. Since then, significant results were registered in achieving more equitable access to formal education. Currently, most of Arab countries register full or close to full enrollment in basic, secondary, and tertiary education equivalent to countries in other regions with similar levels of development. Almost all countries in the region educate their boys and girls at primary level and significant percentage of the relevant age cohorts are

---

29 Abdul Fatah Ali Al-Rashdan, "Higher Education in the Arab World: Hopes and Challenges," http://www.isn.ethz.ch/isn/Digital-Library/Publications/Detail/?ots591=0c54e3b3-1e9c-be1e-2c24-a6a8c7060233&lng=en&id=103115. (Search date: April 11, 2011)

engaged in secondary and tertiary education. Moreover, the region has no longer wide gender disparities in secondary and tertiary education enrollment, and illiteracy rates have been reduced significantly.[30]

The spread of education in the Arab region is mainly characterized by the relatively high spending that was registered since 1960s. Arab governments spent an average of approximately 5% of their GDP on education between 1965 and 2003, whereas East Asian and Latin American countries spent close to 3%.[31] As indicates Table 2.2, most countries - rich and poor - allocated more than 20% of their budgets to education, including, for example, Saudi Arabia, United Arab Emirates, Tunisia, Libya, Algeria, Yemen, and Morocco. A similar number of countries allocate less than 15% of their budget to education, including Oman, Jordan, Lebanon, Bahrain, Kuwait, Syria, Palestine, and Qatar.

---

30 "The Road Not Traveled," *op. cit.*

31 *Ibid.*

Table 2.2: Public Expenditure per Student by Level of Education and Ratio of Expenditure for Secondary/Primary and Tertiary/Primary, 1980-2002

Countries	Primary spending/ pupil 1980	Primary spending/ pupil 2002	Secondary spending/ pupil 2002	Secondary/ primary 2002	Tertiary spending/ student 2002	Tertiary/ secondary 2002
Algeria	493	628	952	1.52	NA	NA
Bahrain	NA	2,620	2,931	1.12	NA	NA
Jordan	NA	596	705	1.18	NA	NA
Kuwait	2,935	2,709	3,336	1.23	NA	NA
Morocco	436	714	1,831	2.56	3,442	1.88
Oman	NA	1,766	2,765	1.57	7,248	2.62
S. Arabia	4,278	3,817	3,749	0.98	NA	NA
Syria	222	477	883	1.85	NA	NA
Tunisia	482	1,000	1,530	1.53	4,065	2.66

Sources: World Bank Central Database and UNESCO Institute for Statistics Statistical Yearbooks2011

The generous spending on education was translated in building schools, hiring teachers and rapidly establishing a great number of universities in recent decades. In 1950, there were no more than ten universities scattered across the region. Today, however, the Arab region has more than 200 higher education institutions, universities, and colleges, and has witnessed an unprecedented increase in enrollment rates.[32] Table 2.3 shows that the percentages

---

32 Ali El-Hawat, "Funding Higher Education in The Arab States: Thoughts and Reflections on the Topic," http://unescore-clic.org/node/114. (Search date: October 11, 2012)

of net enrollment rates in Arab countries have witnessed a tremendous increase in enrollment rates over the period of 1970 - 2003, only Djibouti has achieved low levels. The number of pupils reaching grade five has seen a significant increase in the same period.

Table 2.3: Access to Primary School Education: Net Enrollment Rate, Repetition Rate, and Pupils Reaching Grade Five, 1970–2003

Countries	1970			1985			2003		
	NER	Repetition	Grade 5	NER	Repetition	Grade 5	NER	Repetition	Grade 5
Algeria	76.6	12.5	85.5	86	7.5	93.6	97.1	11.8	94.4
Bahrain	70.6	NA	NA	96.2	8.6	86.5	96.8	3.2	99.9
Djibouti	NA	10.7	81.5	31.3	12.5	91.6	32.9	10.4	NA
Egypt	62.8	4.5	80.6	83.7	1.5	97.4	98.3	4	98.6
Iraq	55.4	20.6	73.7	93.1	20.8	84	87.7	8	NA
Jordan	78.6	4.1	78.9	94.1	5.4	91.2	101.1	0.5	98.8
Lebanon	60.6	15.6	NA	86.7	5.2	NA	86	2.5	NA
Libya	NA	NA	NA	77.8	NA	NA	93.2	10.1	97.6
Morocco	85.7	25.8	90.7	96.1	NA	NA	NA	NA	NA
Oman	39.1	29.8	65.8	60.7	19.8	68.9	92	13.8	75.6
Qatar	27.1	9.3	74	66.4	11.7	93.5	77.9	0.8	97.6
S. Arabia	71.9	23.7	96.7	91.1	10.7	98.8	89.8	NA	NA
Syria	32.4	15.2	82.6	50.9	12.4	93.3	53.1	4.2	93.6
Tunisia	69.5	10.9	88.9	94.7	7.5	95.5	98.1	7.5	***
U. A. E.	75.6	29.2	67.8	93.1	20.4	86.6	97.2	9.2	96.5
Palestine	NA	15.2	99.7	76.5	5.7	87.9	71.2	2.2	94.7
Yemen	NA	NA	NA	NA	NA	NA	86.36	0.2	NA

Sources: World Bank Central Database and UNESCO Institute for Statistics Statistical Yearbooks2011

Table 2.4: Gross Enrollment Rates in Secondary and Tertiary Education, 1970–2003 (percent)

Countries	1970		1985		2003	
	Secondary	Tertiary	Secondary	Tertiary	Secondary	Tertiary
Algeria	11.2	1.8	51.4	7.9	80.7	19.6
Bahrain	51.3	1.4	97.2	12.8	98.8	34.4
Djibouti	6.6	NA	11.7	NA	21.5	1.6
Egypt	28.4	6.9	61.4	18.1	871	32.6
Iraq	24.4	4.8	53.8	11.5	42.0	15.4
Jordan	32.8	2.1	52.2	13.1	87.4	39.3
Lebanon	41.5	21.0	60.6	27.8	88.7	47.6
Libya	20.8	2.9	58.8	9.2	103.9	56.2
Morocco	12.6	1.4	35.4	8.7	47.6	10.6
Oman	0	NA	26.5	0.8	86.4	12.9
Qatar	36.3	4.5	82.3	20.7	96.8	19.1
S. Arabia	12.1	1.6	40.1	10.6	67.8	27.7
Syria	38.1	8.3	58.2	17.1	63.2	NA
Tunisia	22.7	2.6	38.9	5.5	81.3	28.6
UAE	21.8	NA	54.7	6.8	66.5	22.5
Palestine	NA	NA	NA	NA	93.6	37.9
Yemen	NA	NA	NA	NA	45.9	13.2

Sources: World Bank Central Database and UNESCO Institute for Statistics Statistical Yearbooks2011

The majority of young boys and girls are now educated at the primary level in most Arab countries. Similar progress has been made with respect to the proportion of the age cohort attending secondary school and university. The Arab region was able to mark an almost threefold increase in enrollment at the secondary school level between 1970 and 2003; and approximately a fivefold one at the level of higher education as shown in Table 2.4. Between 1960 and 2000, the average number of years of schooling of the adult population (15 years and above) in the Arab region grew faster than in other regions of the world.[33]

Arab countries have made significant progress in reducing illiteracy and increasing educational attainments over the past 30 years.[34] In Egypt, the share of the population aged 15 years and older that could read and write surged from 40% to 83% between 1980 and 2004, thanks to educational expansion at the primary level. Morocco also achieved notable improvements in literacy from 29% to 52%. Girls now enroll in primary school at almost the same rate as boys, and an increasing number of young women are entering universities, in some countries even outnumbering male students. In 1990, gross enrolment rates at tertiary level were higher for men than for women in all countries except Jordan, Kuwait and Qatar.[35]

---

[33] "The Road Not Traveled Education Reform in the Middle East and North Africa," http://siteresources.worldbank.org/INTMENA/Resources/EDU_Flagship_ Full_ENG.pdf. (Search date: September 11, 2011)

[34] *Ibid.*

[35] *Ibid.*

Even though the Arab region registered a rapid improvement of its educational system with enrollment rates increasing by 85% from 1975 to 1991, the level of illiteracy among the adult population, especially among women, sharply distinguishes most Arab countries from most Latin American and East Asian societies. In two countries, Morocco and Yemen, about one half of the population remains illiterate. The total number of illiterates in Arab countries (54 million) represents about 1.5% of all illiterate adults in the world. The 36 million illiterate women in Arab region also represent about 2.2% of all illiterate women in the world.

Despite the relatively high illiteracy rates among adults, most Arab countries have achieved high levels of literacy among youth (15- 24 years) in the last two decades, reaching unprecedented levels in Arab countries. Bahrain 100%, Libya 99.9%, Jordan 98.9%, Kuwait 98.4%, Oman, Qatar, Saudi Arabia 98%, Tunisia 96.8%, and Syria 94.4%. Other countries have achieved relatively high levels, Egypt 84.9%, Yemen 84.1%; meanwhile Mauritania and Morocco have registered very low literacy rates among the Arab countries with 67.7% and 79.9% respectively.

Female literacy has been increasing among youth, and the rate of change has been rapid and steady.[36]

The Arab region has made remarkable progress in the last 30 years with respect to closing the gender gap in education. Progress has been quick and constant, covering all levels of education. Although the region started with relatively low levels of gender parity, the parity indices for secondary and higher education are not significantly different from the corresponding indices for Latin America and East Asia. The area where more progress is still needed is in relation to illiteracy, which remains significant among the female adult population, as discussed in the section on education quality.[37]

Progress has not been even across all counties, however, with respect to primary education, Yemen has yet to close the gender gap. At the level of secondary education, although few countries have attained full secondary enrollment, almost all have attained gender parity. Only

---

[36] Nader Fergany, "Arab Higher Education and Development: An Overview," http://www.ties-project.eu/sites/uni4inno.eu/files/Arab%20 HE%20and%20 development.pdf. (Search date: July 22, 2011)

[37] "The Road Not Traveled," *op. cit.*

Iraq, Morocco, and Yemen still have significant secondary education gender gaps. Furthermore, for Algeria, Bahrain, Jordan, Kuwait, Lebanon, Libya, Tunisia, and the United Arab Emirates the gender gap at secondary levels is smaller than at primary levels. Gender parity rates for higher education are even higher than they are for secondary education in most Arab countries. In fact, only in Iraq, and Yemen does the proportion of male students significantly surpass that of females. In Algeria, Bahrain, Iran, Jordan, Kuwait, Lebanon, Libya, Oman, Qatar, Saudi Arabia, Tunisia, the United Arab Emirates, and Palestine, female students outnumber male students, and most countries achieved gender parity during the 1990s.[38]

Higher education has expanded rapidly in the Arab region as a recent phenomenon. It is often alleged that rapid expansion in education, especially the higher variety, inevitably entails some trade off between quality and quantity, meaning that rapid quantitative expansion in higher education can only come at the expense of quality.[39] According to an analysis of the World Bank, in

---

38 "The Road Not Traveled," *op. cit.*

39 Ali El-Hawat, *op. cit.*

most Arab countries, works with little or no educational backgrounds, and those with post secondary education, constitute smaller share of unemployment. Most of the unemployed are either semi-skilled or have attained intermediate or secondary education levels.[40]

Arab countries have registered tremendous success in terms of providing free access to education, bridging the gender gap, increasing literacy rates especially among youth. They also witnessed massive increases in newly built schools and universities, generously spent, relatively, high percentage of their GDP and annual government budgets on education. But the problem is the quality of education, because the attention was more on spreading education quantitatively. Less funding was given to higher education, which affects the quality of programs and university outcomes. Students graduate lacking skills needed in the market, perhaps the most striking characteristics of university graduates is the low level of knowledge attainment, weak analytical and innovative abilities and steady deterioration of both.

---

[40] "Unlocking the Employment," *op. cit.*

2.4. The Common Characteristics of the Uprisings

The Arab Spring uprisings share many common characteristics, namely leaderless, non-ideological, youth-driven, pivotal role of women, the use of media and social networks, and similar slogans chanted over the Arab streets.

2.4.1. Leaderless Uprisings

Usually revolutions have a clear leadership to give instructions and lead rebellions with working plans and defined targets. However, the Arab Spring was initiated by young activists, which led many of anti-political actions without the intervention of traditional opposition forces. The reason behind the absence of leadership is the sudden outbreak of these uprisings, the lack of a credible opposition, and the tight control exercised by the regimes over political parties and civil society. As people gathered in the streets and public squares, activists started working on the ground. For example in Egypt, near Tahrir Square in Cairo, young activists improvised an operation center in an abandoned touristic company where they "received journalists and gave orders to the youth in the field."[41]

Some argue that, in spite of its diversity and complexity, the Arab Spring can be encapsulated in one very expressive and politically charged concept which has been absent from the political arena for too long: "the people."[42] It started in Tunisia, under the slogan adopted by the Tunisian demonstrators in the earliest beginnings of their popular uprising: *"if the people one day decide to live, destiny will respond."*[43] Since then, the spirit of the slogan has been adopted by all the Arab uprisings. The same slogan was chanted by young Tunisians, Egypt, Yemeni, Libyans, and Syrians: *'The people want to overthrow the regime'*, while Moroccans, Jordanians, and Bahrainis (in the beginning) demanded political reform rather than

---

[41] Vicken Cheterian, "The Arab Revolt: Roots and Perspectives," http://www.isn.ethz.ch/isn/Digital-Library/Publications/Detail/?ots591=0c54e3b3-1e9c-be1e-2c2a6a8c7060233&lng=en&id=127332. (Search date: September 11, 2012)

[42] Mohamed Ali Atassi, "What People Want," Doreen Khoury, Anbara Abu-Ayyash, and Joachim Paul (eds.) (2011), *op. cit.*, p. 28.

[43] An Excerpt From A Famous Poem By Tunisian Poet Abul-Qasim Al-Shabi, Written in the 1930s in the midst of the Tunisian struggle against colonialism.

regime change emphasizing that the absolute monarchy should be reformed.

The 'people' is a key term, and can be used to analyze the uprisings that have shaken the whole Arab world. Adopting this term by the demonstrators and repeating it over and over again in the many different versions of the slogans and demands spreading across the Arab world, means that individuals who have been deprived for many decades not only of their right to participate in the political affairs, but also of their most basic rights. Popular movements played a crucial role in organizing demonstrations in the Arab Spring countries. In Egypt, the 'April 6' movement was the main movement that organized demonstrations. However, in Syria, the iron grip of the security services made mobilization by organized groups completely impossible. Therefore, demonstrations have spontaneously appeared in different areas of Syrian cities, without prior planning from a national leadership, and demonstrators created the Syrian Revolution Coordinators Union to coordinate. The Arab Spring lacked leadership, as well as a defined and unified ideology while the only aim was regime change or regime reform.[44]

2.4.2. The Lack of a Unifying Ideology

People from different political, social, and religious backgrounds spontaneously took to the streets, gathered in public squares, and chanted the same slogans. Although Political Islam parties were the main beneficiaries of the post-Arab spring uprisings they were neither the initiators nor the galvanizers of the uprisings in their early stages. Their tardiness to join the demonstrations can be understood as a way to escape the iron grip of the stale regimes, and to avoid being taken as a scapegoat to crack down the blooming revolts.

Arab rebels chanted the same slogans across the region from Morocco to Syria: regime change / reform, freedom, dignity, and justice. For example, in Egypt, the 18 days massive protests of an estimated 12 million people, which

---

[44] Radwan Ziadeh, "The Syrian Revolution: The Role of the Emerging Leaders," Stephen Zunes et al., *Revolution and Political Transformation in the Middle East* (*Washington* D.C: Middle East Institute, 2011), p. 44.

is perhaps the largest civil insurrection in history, of ordinary Egyptians, men and women, Christians and Muslims, young and old, workers and intellectuals, poor and middle classes, secular and religious walked side by side and faced together truncheons, tear gas, water cannons, and bullets for their freedom.[45] In general, the young educated generation from different political, religious, ethnical, and social backgrounds gathered for the sake of their nations.

2.4.3. Educated Youth-driven Uprisings

The youth-led uprisings that swept the Arab world in 2011 have refocused the world's attention on the region's 100 million strong young population and its critical role in driving a decisive change in the existing political, economic, and social structures in the Arab world. Arab youth under the age of 25 represent an estimated and unprecedented 60% of the region's population. They have raised expectations for themselves and for their societies,

---

45 Stephen Zunes, "The Power of Strategic Nonviolent Action in Arab Revolutions," Stephen Zunes et al. (2011), *op. cit.*, p. 11.

but the main constraint was economic and political realities. For years, scholars have been warning that the disproportionately large population of young people in the Arab world is a ticking bomb, young educated men with little access to jobs are more likely to join rebel movements, if not easily recruited by fanatical groups.[46] The educated class, students, and unemployed university graduates were the engine of the uprisings that swept most of the Arab countries.

The Arab Spring occurred in the time of amazing educational achievements that the region has witnessed amid high spending on education. The Arab region spent about 5% of GDP and 20% of government budgets in education over the past decades, and made tremendous gains in education attainment and combating illiteracy as a result. These formidable results have embarked it on a cultural and mental revolution that paves the way towards democracy. The combination of population awareness resulted from the spread of education, mainly among youth sparked the uprisings, and the rising rates

---

[46] Stephanie Schwartz, "Youth and the "Arab Spring," http://www.usip.org/publications/youth-and-the-arab-spring. (Search date: November 11, 2012)

of unemployment among educated youth, mainly university graduates, fueled and assured their spread and continuity. An educated generation sparked the uprisings using Internet and social media to mobilize mass population, and unemployed university graduates fueled the demonstrations through the Arab streets to end up with the Arab Spring. [47]

This young generation is best understood as a global generation, which share three core characteristics. First, a deep sense of ownership over the change they have created across the Arab region. Second, a feeling of connectivity that includes but is not limited to social media, this connection was seen in the ground where demonstrators were working together regardless of their religious, political, or ethnical background. Third, a strong sense of global citizenship, itself a product of technological change and expanding networks of communication. They were thinking globally and acting

---

[47] Kevin Watkins, "Education Failures Fan the Flames in The Arab World," http://efareport.wordpress.com/2011/02/23/education-failures-fan-the-flames-in-the-arab-world. (Search date: September 12, 2012)

locally, the social media was their way to communicate with each other and to share with the world.[48]

2.4.4. Social Media for Mass Mobilization

Social media is playing a crucial role in connecting people and bringing together disparate groups and individuals to support a common cause across vast areas in the world. The role of social media during the Arab Spring uprisings was to facilitate and speed up the disintegration of at least two regimes in Tunisia and Egypt, and a prominent role in mobilizing mass population in Bahrain and Syria. Before the outbreak of the Arab Spring, social media played an important role of exposing the regime abuses and getting around censorship. As the uprisings took place, social media become a tool of coordination for timing the protests, sharing demonstrations and police abuses with the world, and supporting each other in different countries. One

---

[48] Steve Coll, "The Second Tunisian Revolution: A New Model of Change For A New Generation," http://www.usmep.us/usmep/wp-content/uploads/2011-18-USMEPolicy-Brief1.pdf. (Search date: September 17, 2012)

must be careful not to overstate the role of social media; it was only a tool for mass mobilization.[49]

In Egypt, the protests started by a Facebook campaign run by the 'April 6 Youth Movement,' and 'We Are All Khalid Said,' which "generated tens of thousands of positive responses to the call to rally against government policies. The profile of the most active users, young, urban, and relatively educated, fully corresponds to the core of the first anti-government protesters in January that later led to a larger and more mass-based campaign. Overall, the input of the social media networks was critical in performing two overlapping functions, organizing the protests, and disseminating information about them, including publicizing protesters' demands internationally (Facebook reportedly outmatched Al Jazeera in at least the speed of news dissemination)."[50]

---

49 Ekaterina Stepanova, "The Role of Information Communication Technologies in the Arab Spring: Implications Beyond The Region," http://www.gwu.edu/~ieresgwu/assets/docs/ponars.pepm_159.pdf. (Search date: September 27, 2012)

50 Steve Morris, "Using Digital and Social Media During A Crisis Tackling The Proliferation of New Communications Channels," http://www.portland-communications.com/using-digital-and-social-media-during-crisis. (Search date: September 17, 2012)

What indicates that social media was only a facilitator is that states with some of the highest levels of Internet usage, such as Bahrain with 88% of its population online, and states with some of the lowest levels of Internet exposure like Yemen and Libya, both experienced mass protests. But what can be registered about Libya is that the literacy rates are high, and in Yemen, the spread of education witnessed a significant progress lately. This indicates that the absence or the low use of social media networks as direct facilitators in organizing protests did not diminish the role of mainstream electronic media devices. Cell phones, tweets, emails, and video clips, were capable of quickly capturing and broadly transmitting eyewitness accounts of domestic developments to the rest of the world.[51]

2.4.5. Nonviolent Uprisings

What characterized the Arab Spring early 2011 was its nonviolent movements, where tens of thousands of people flooded to the streets shouting 'Salmiya

---

[51] Steve Morris, *op. cit.*

Salmiya,'[peaceful in Arabic] even when they were under gunfire in most of the countries. These nonviolent pro-democracy insurrections succeeded in reshaping the area in very a short time; tore the walls of fear that dominated the region for decades, toppled presidents, and seriously challenged kings.[52] During the 2000s, many nonviolent revolutions took place in the world, starting with the Serbian revolution in 2000, the color Revolution in Eastern Europe, Georgia and Ukraine, and the Cedar Revolution in Lebanon.

The choice of nonviolence means that the Arab revolutions were not centered primarily on an ethical commitment to nonviolence as much as it was the recognition that nonviolent methods were most effective strategically. Even in the cases of Libya and Syria, they started as nonviolent movements calling for freedom, justice, and dignity. Similarly in Yemen, with the exception of one tribal faction and some mutinous military groupings, the pro-democracy protests have been

---

52 Michael Shank, "How the Arab Spring Sprung From a Nonviolent Source," http://www.huffingtonpst.com/michael-shank/arab-spring-source_b_974836.html. (Search date: April 11, 2012)

remarkably nonviolent, particularly given that Yemen is one of the most heavily armed countries in the world in terms of individual gun ownership, with some estimates as high as three weapons per person. The fact that the millions of Yemenis who have taken to the streets have consciously left their weapons at home and largely maintained a strict nonviolent discipline is nothing short of remarkable.[53]

2.4.6. Women's Pivotal Role

Women in Tunisia, Egypt, Yemen, and Libya have played a frontline role in bringing down entrenched dictatorships. Female voices rang out loud and clear during the massive protests sweeping Arab streets. Arab Spring revealed many females' activist names as Asmaa Mahfouz, Tawakoul Karman, Lina Ben Mhenni, and others that had an enormous role in these uprisings in many countries across the area.

In Egypt, Among the names that shaped the Egyptian revolution, Asmaa Mahfouz, a young Egyptian woman

---

[53] Michael Shank, *op. cit.*

who launched a video blog calling Egyptian people to rise up against Mubarak's regime before the outbreak of January 25th Uprising, her video became a viral hit. During the uprising women were beside men throwing stones, moving dead bodies, they did everything, in the ground there was no difference between men and women, they were all working for Egypt. She is widely credited with having inspired Egyptians to take to the streets in defiance of a long-running autocratic regime. In her video, to galvanize people to take to the streets, she said that the only way to live in dignity to rise up and to overthrow the regime, "Whoever says women shouldn't protest should be man enough to come with me on January 25."[54]

In Tunisia, Lina Ben Mhenni, an activist, she is running a blog 'A Tunisian Girl,' where her posts were documenting the protests in her travels across the country. Besides photographing the dead and wounded, she included pictures of herself with male protesters at sit-ins in the Kasbah in Tunis, during the revolution days. Lina is

---

[54] Natacha Yazbeck, "In Arab Revolts, Women Emerge as Driving Force," http://www.thejakartaglobe.com/international/in-arab-revolts-women-emerge-as-driving-force/427281. (Search date: September 12, 2012)

only one example of hundreds if not thousands of Tunisian women who rose up against tyranny beside men seeking change for a better future.

In Yemen, Tawakul Karman, a human rights activist, awarded the Nobel peace prize at the beginning of October 2011, has been a leading figure in the pro-democracy demonstrations, camping out for months in front of Sana'a University, calling for Saleh to step down. Defying their stereotype as victims of oppressive patriarchies, Arab women have made their presence a defining feature of the Arab spring.[55]

The role of women was also crucial in Bahrain, a country that has witnessed a sectarian split between Shia and Sunni. During the Bahraini uprising, the participation of women was notable in demanding political reforms and freedom, and other supported the regime policies as well and openly expressed their loyalty.[56] Unprecedentedly, women played and continue to play an imminent role in

---

[55] "Women and The Arab Awakening Now is the Time," http://www.economist.com/node/21532256. (Search date: August 11, 2012)

[56] Jumana Al Tamimi, "Women fuel Arab revolts," http://gulfnews.com/news/region/women-fuel-arab-revolts-1.772905. (Search date: September 15, 2012)

the Arab Spring uprisings, and expected to play more roles in the coming waves of uprisings that will hit the region. The role of women in these uprisings indicates that women empowerment is taking place in the region due to the spread of education among females. In 2002 Arab Human Development Report[57] published by United Nations Development Programme (UNDP), women empowerment, education, and freedom were three deficits of the region. A decade later, the role of women was pivotal in freedom movements driven by educated young generation.

---

57 "Creating Opportunities for Future Generations," http://www.arab-hdr.org/publications/other/ahdr/ahdr2002e.pdf. (Search date: November 21, 2012)

• *Chapter III* •

The Arab Spring and Education

Is it important to mention that education is an important element for the use of social media and for understanding TV programs, which are delivered in Arabic. Unlike other places in the world, in the Arab countries the spoken languages are different from the written. The Arab region from North West Africa to West Asia shares the same mother language, Arabic *Fos'ha* (formal Arabic), which is the official language of 22 Arab countries. But each country uses its own dialect as a spoken language, which is more or less far from the formal Arabic. Sometimes the communication between

Arabs is quiet difficult when using their local dialects, which means that the only way to understand each other, is by using formal Arabic or other foreign languages to communicate. People who have the ability to use and understand the formal Arabic are literate people, since it is taught only in regular or traditional schools. This means, that the new Arab public sphere would not take place unless there is a certain level of education among the Arab youth to communicate, as well as to be able to use the new technologies.

The role of education is crucial in understanding the mainstream media and the usage of Internet, because they require the ability to read and write to have access to websites to understand the discussion in the forums and blogs and the mainstream media. Understanding the issues of human rights, freedom, social justice, and democracy requires higher levels of education, since the authoritarian regimes implanted, through public education and their media, the inability of the Arab region to adopt Western democracy because of the political culture of the area. The usage of Internet does not require only the ability of reading and writing in Arabic but also the knowledge of foreign languages, mainly English or French.

The use of Internet was very scarce early 2000s, and most of people did not have access to it, or even had a personal computer. For example, less than 15% of the Egyptians had access to Internet (mostly through cyber cafes heavily policed by the regime).[58] Moreover, the use of Internet in some Arab Spring countries was low in the eve of the outbreak of the Arab uprisings. For example, Libya's use of Internet was 5.9%, Yemen 1.6%, and Syria 19.6% of the total population. The low access to Internet indicates that the role of social media is not a trigger of the uprisings rather than a facilitator for mobilizing mass population. Al-Qaeda used social media to recruit and share news and communicate within its networks across the world. It is the same way social media is used during the uprisings to galvanize mass population to peacefully protest.

---

[58] Stephan Zunes, "The Power of Strategic nonviolent Action in Arab Revolution," Stephan Zunes et al., *Revolution and Political Transformation in the Middle East* (Washington: The Middle East Institute, 2011), p. 11.

Information and communication networks can serve as powerful accelerators of social transformation. The new tools of social media have reinvented social activism. With Facebook and Twitter and other Social Networking Services (SNS), the traditional relationship between political authority and people's will has been upended, making it easier for the powerless to collaborate, coordinate, and give voice to their concerns. The civil rights movements, which took place in the US in 1960s, used the available tools to spread across the US. Taking the 2000s revolutions, starting with Yugoslavia in 2000, and the use of social networking tools was a way to facilitate the mobilization. Phone messages played a decisive role in changing the mainstream opinion in Spain in 2004 in the eve of parliament elections. In Moldova, a country where very few Twitter accounts exist a revolution took place. Social networking services were facilitating factors and the Arab spring uprisings came in the same process.[59]

---

[59] Malcolm Gladwell, "Small Change: Why the Revolution Will Not be Tweeted," http://www.newyorker.com/reporting/2010/10/04/101004fa_fact _ gladwell?currentPage=all. (Search date: November 12, 2012)

The role that media is playing in the age of revolutions, is bringing together disparate groups, creating communication channels far from being controlled by states. Social media is important because it is an ideal tool for connecting loose networks of association, bringing together otherwise disparate groups and individuals to support a common cause. Today's digital tools are the Internet (for information dissemination and news), social media (to connect and coordinate), mobile phones (to capture what happens) and digital, particularly satellite, television to report it. These tools have no respect to borders, what happens in Morocco and Egypt motivates and empowers protesters in Libya, Syria and Yemen.[60]

Moreover, the use of Internet in some Arab Spring countries was low in the eve of the outbreak of the Arab uprisings. For example, Libya's use of Internet was 5.9%, Yemen 1.6%, and Syria 19.6% of the total population. The use of Internet tools was only a way of mobilization and communication as once printer played a role in the

---

[60] Andy Williamson, "Social Media and the New Arab Spring," http://www.hansardsociety.org.uk/blogs/edemocracy/archive/2011/04/19/social-media-and-the-new-arab-spring.aspx. (Search date: November 15, 2012)

French Revolution, Radio tapes in the Iranian Revolution and SMS texts in the Serbian Revolution. Kefaya Movement was at the core of change that has occurred in Egypt, was established in 2004 by educated people mainly youth from different political and religious trends. Later, it gave birth to April 6 Movement that mobilized people to take to streets demanding freedom, dignity, and justice.

Arguing Western powers' intention to change the Arab regimes through popular uprisings is far away from providing a rational argument, because Western powers were taken by surprise as the Jasmine revolution broke out in Tunisia, and the quick collapse of Ben Ali's regime. The French Minister of Foreign Affairs resigned because of her open support to the Tunisian president during the uprising. The same support was also given to Mubarak in Egypt and to Saleh and Yemen. Saudi Arabia was given green light to intervene militarily in Bahrain to restore the seriously challenged monarchy.

The Algerian Lesson is still present in the minds of Western powers. In early 1990s, Algeria was swept by a popular unrest, which led to a revised constitution, political open up, and transition to multiparty system. In the spring of 1991, on the eve of the spectacular victory in parliamentary elections of the Islamic Salvation Front (Islamist party), the military called off the democratic transition and staged a coup d'état. They banned the Islamist party, jailed its leadership, and drove Algeria into the Black Decade of Civil War. The lesson learnt from the Algerian experience, was not only the abhorred regimes lack any popularity, but also free election will pave the way for Islamists to power. It was also obvious that the Arab despots who are the best guarantors of Western interests in an unpredictable region.[61] A fake version of democracy was promoted, cosmetic elections were held, and the old tyrants made significant efforts to organize referendums where they barely could reach 99.99% as single candidates. Fraudulent elections, in favor of the de facto unique party or pro-regimes parties symbolized the post-Cold War Arab World.

The European and later the American intervention in the Arab region played a major role in all the transformations that the area passed through since the

---

[61] Peter Mansfield, *op. cit.*, p. 414.

collapse of the Ottoman Empire. After the European colonialism redrew the fault lines and contours of the new area, which was reshaped by the Cold War with the United States at the helm of interregional and even domestic affairs of most Arab countries. The United States, guided by imperial security doctrines, put itself center-stage as the most powerful player in the Middle East and gave its full support to tyrant regimes in the regimes.[62]

In 2004, when Ben Ali was in a visit to the White House, Bush praised him as an ally in the war on terrorism, as well as his political reforms, press freedom, and free elections. Ben Ali is only an example of the way the US is dealing with its allies who, in return, provide implicit and explicit support for the American policies in the region. Bush declaration that the Middle East will remain a place of stagnation, resentment, and violence ready for export as long as it is immune to democracy, was only an exercise of pressure on Arab regimes to support his plans on invading Iraq back then.

---

[62] Marwan Bishara, "In the Arab World: The West's Interests Trump its Values," http://www.aljazeera.com/indepth/opinion/2012/02/201221412121 0448673.html. (Search date: November 14, 2012)

Many would argue that Bush's intention to democratize the Arab region was because of its involvement in September 11 terrorists attack. Yet, the US never intended to democratize the region, and even the invasion of Iraq, which was under the name of democratizing the country, it was clear that dominating its natural resources was the main reason for the invasion. By 2004, pressures were exercised on Palestine to democratize, which was coincided with Bush Initiative for the Greater Middle East. As Hamas won the elections, it was boycotted and Palestine entered into an era of internal instability and political division between the president and the elected government.

Later, "the Egyptian elections of 2005 and 2006 were rigged. The majority of the elected Hamas parliament members ended up in jail, and its government was toppled with the complicity of the Bush administration. The elections in Saudi Arabia were merely municipal and totally apolitical. The implementation of the 'democracy agenda' was carried on the backs of tanks and aircraft carriers that destroyed Iraq, tore up its national fabric, inflamed hatreds, and ultimately, exacerbated anti-

Americanism, while weakening the secular, liberal trend in the region and causing the death of at least one hundred thousand Iraqis."[63]

The socio-economic inequalities are not the result of the last decade or the past few years to be considered as the main factors that have caused the Arab Spring uprisings, although their role as facilitators in fueling the uprisings is undeniable. The Arab region witnessed an economic downturn since 1980s, where GDP growth per worker in the region was less than 1 % per year, and modest gains in human capital were largely offset by a continuous decline in total factor productivity in 1980s and 1990s.[64] During the 1960s and 1970s much of the Arab world, pursued ambitious state-driven economic strategies, which, by the mid-eighties, were generating only modest economic results and proving fiscally unsustainable. These events led to what was known as *'bread riots'* that started from Tunisia 1984.

---

[63] Marwan Bishara, *op. cit.*

[64] Tarik M. Yousef, "Development, Growth and Policy Reform in the Middle East and North Africa Since 1950," *Journal of Economic Perspectives*, Vol. 18, No. 3 (Summer 2004), p. 91.

The economic downturn then further aggravated the economies of the region and faced with vast deficits and high levels of debt and inflation. These countries were forced to seek help from the World Bank (WB) and the International Monetary Fund (IMF). Since then, they have pursued series of market-oriented reforms with the objective of limiting the state's intervention in the economy, promoting private sector growth and integrating their economies into the world market. These policies imposed by WB and IMF had negative repercussions on the social and economic situation, and the economies have continued to suffer from structural fragilities and weaknesses.

Education has contributed as a fundamental factor in galvanizing the Arab population to raise their voice against injustice and seek democracy and social justice. The demands that were raised through the Arab streets were not economic demands in basic, but mainly political demands concerning regime change, freedom, dignity, and social justice. These demands can be rooted in the writings of European Renaissance literature of social contract of John Locke and Jean-Jacques Rousseau and others, and civil state of Charles Des Montesquieu.

The Arab Spring prodemocracy movements in 2011 raised demands of regime change in Tunisia, Egypt, Yemen, Bahrain, and Syria, and sought freedom, dignity, and social justice. Educated people with certain knowledge of democracy, political understanding, and human rights raised these demands and not only unemployed and jobless youth. These uprisings were leaderless and no defined and unified ideology. Most of the young activists are well educated from the middle class. Indeed Arab Spring uprisings were fueled by unemployed youth, but the main figures of these uprisings were from prosperous families.

For example, Weal Ghonim a Dubai-based Google executive, was an icon of the Egyptian uprising, as well as other Egyptian activists were mainly from middle class families. Most of Arab activists, who played important roles in triggering the uprisings and galvanized ordinary people to take to the streets were lawyers, university professors, and even university students. Unemployment rate in Arab countries 32%, which is the same in Sub-

Saharan African countries, even the latter are much bigger in number and population. 35% of people in the Arab countries are employed for year for an employer; they have a stable work, while 22% for Sub-Saharan countries.[65]

High unemployment rate among youth is an impending threat to stability in Africa. This concern is certainly valid as Africa's youth population (15–24 year olds) has been increasing faster than in any other part of the world. According to the World Bank, 200 million people in Africa fall into this category, making up 20% of the population, 40% of the work force, and 60% of the unemployed on the continent. A large portion of people aged 15–24 in Sub-Saharan Africa are involved in self-employment in the informal and agricultural sectors. For example, 94% of the total population in Mali, 74% in Ethiopia, and 31% in South Africa are employed in the informal sector. However, employment for the 15–24 age

---

[65] Jenny Marlar, "Global Unemployment at 8% in 2011: Youth are Three Times More Likely Than Older Adults to be Unemployed," http://www.gallup.com/poll/153884/global-unemployment-2011.aspx. (Search date: December 21, 2012)

portion, compared to the total population, has remained largely stagnant despite that this age group is increasing in size. This means that more and more youth are not fully absorbed in the economy or making significant increases in income, in self-employment or in agriculture.[66]

The conventional wisdom, since at least the writings of John Dewey (1916), views high levels of educational attainment as a prerequisite for democracy. Education is argued to promote democracy both because it enables a 'culture of democracy' to develop and because it leads to greater prosperity, which is also thought to cause political development. Based on this, we argue that education had a pivotal contribution in the outbreak in the Arab Spring prodemocracy movements, mainly among youth. The educated youth succeeded in mobilizing, nonviolently, mass population across the Arab streets using social networking platforms to demonstrate in the urban centers for more freedom and against despotism. The demands

---

[66] Julius Agbor, Olumide Taiwo and Jessica Smith, "Sub-Saharan Africa's Youth Bulge: A Demographic Dividend or Disaster?" http://www.brookings.edu/~/media/research/files/reports/2012/1/priorities%20foresight%20africa/01_youth_bulge_agbor_taiwo_smith. (Search date: December 19, 2012)

that were raised during the Arab spring demonstrations reflected the level of the demonstrators. They shouted the same slogans from Casablanca to Damascus: 'freedom, dignity, and social justice,' and regime change or political reform.

Historically, students, as an educated portion of the population, stood behind many revolutions and uprisings throughout the history. They drove riots against authoritarianism in Oxford, Bologna, and Paris in the middle Ages, and they led liberal movements and revolutions in Europe mid-19th century. Students' movements also played a pivotal role in overthrowing many regimes around the world, in Argentina in 1955, Venezuela in 1958, Vietnam in 1963, and Pakistan in 1969. They were also behind many governments step-down; they forced Kishi government to resign in Japan in 1960, and anti-Sukarno movement in 1966. Students were the driving force of 1956 Polish demonstrations, and Hungarian Revolution, 1968 Prague Spring, and 1989 China Tiananmen uprising. In 2000s colored Revolutions, students played important role. Otpor students' movement played an important role in toppling Milosevic regime in 2000, and in the Ukrainian Revolution in 2004 students played a big role.[67]

In the Arab region, education has reached unprecedented levels, where Arab countries have registered tremendous gains in terms of more equitable access to formal education. They registered full or close to full enrollment in basic education, secondary and tertiary rates equivalent to countries in other regions at comparable levels of development. Moreover, the region has almost bridged the gender gap in secondary and tertiary education. Arab region did well on spending on education as a proportion of GDP. In the period of 1965-2003, Middle East and North African (MENA) governments spent an average of approximately 5% of their GDP on education, whereas East Asian and Latin American countries spent closer to 3% of their GDP. In terms of public expenditure per pupil, MENA countries also spent an average more per student at all levels of

---

67 Edward Glaeser, Giacomo Ponzetto, and Andrei Shleifer, "Why Does Democracy Need Education?" *Journal of Economic Growth*, Vol. 12, No. 2 (2007), p. 78.

education than did their comparators sample of East Asia and Latin America.[68]

Education is provided for free in most of the Arab countries since their independence, and the constitutions not only guarantee the right of education to all citizens, but also to be provided free of charge. Free education is provided through all levels of education from primary to tertiary education, and even in some countries some financial support is given to students like in Morocco. These constitutional commitments were made typically in the wake of independence from colonial powers and have put pressure on governments to deliver. This made it very impossible for these governments to stop providing free education for their population. In recent years, however, most countries are increasingly relying on the private sector for the provision of education from pre-primary to tertiary education, while public sector is still providing free education.[69]

Arab countries differ among themselves in the level of the spread of education. Meanwhile Bahrain, Tunisia,

---

68 "The Road Not Traveled, *op. cit.*

69 *Ibid.*

Saudi Arabia and Egypt, and Jordan have achieved high levels of education; Morocco, Yemen, Mauritania, and Sudan registered lower results, although Morocco and Yemen have made significant progress since 1990s. The free access to education, and the unprecedented levels of educational attainments that the region has accumulated, have contributed to the birth of a new educated generation with new hopes for a better future. This educated youth, which galvanized people to take to the streets to change the political *status quo* in their respective countries. As the educated population sparked the uprisings, young unemployed mainly university graduates fueled them.

The combination of awareness and the rising unemployment rates among educated people and mainly university graduates,[70] which was the result of the spread of education, has led to the outbreak of the Arab uprisings. It assured its sustainability and success in overthrowing

---

70 "Unlocking the Employment Potential in the Middle East and North Africa Toward a New Social Contract," http://web.worldbank.org/WBSITE/EXTERNAL/COUNTRIES/MENAEXT/0.contentMDK:20260961~pagePK:146736~piPK:146830~theSitePK:256299,00.html. (Search date: September 11, 2011)

presidents of Tunisia, Egypt, Yemen, and Libya, seriously challenged the monarchy of Bahrain, and launching a bloody revolution in Syria. An educated generation sparked the uprisings using media and social networking services to mobilize mass population, and unemployed university graduates fueled the demonstrations through the Arab Streets to end up with the birth of the Arab Spring as the former Tunisian dictator fled the country under the pressure of heavy demonstrations in January 14, 2011.

The low levels of education in the Arab region were behind the failure of many uprisings in the previous decades. Arab people rose up frequently since early1960s, Morocco 1965, 1981, 1984, 1990; Egypt 1977, 1984, 2008; Tunisia 1984, 2008; Algeria 1984, 1988; Jordan 2005, and political instability in Bahrain since its independence and mainly since 2001. All of these previous uprisings failed to seriously challenge the dictatorship. We presume that the role of education was decisive in the success and failure of these uprisings. The previous uprisings did not succeed because the level of education among the population was low, and the 2011 uprisings succeeded in mobilizing mass population and toppling repressive regimes of Tunisia, Egypt, Libya, and Yemen because education reached unprecedented levels.

The role of education is crucial in understanding the mainstream media, since TV programs, especially Al-Jazeera, are diffused in formal Arabic, which only educated, or at least literate people can understand them. The usage of Internet requires the ability to read and write to have access to websites, to understand the discussion in the forums and blogs. Understanding the issues of human rights, freedom, social justice, and democracy requires higher levels of education, since the authoritarian regimes implanted through public education and media the inability of the Arab region to adopt Western democracy because of the political culture of the area. The usage of Internet does not require only the ability to read and write Arabic but also the knowledge of other foreign languages, mainly English and French.

Education is the fundamental factor that made Arab population, mainly youth, aware that the dictatorship is the source of economic and political failures, Arab defeats, and Arab humiliations. This educated generation was able to compare their countries with Asian countries, which were poor only few decades back, when Arab region was enjoying a better situation. Early 1960s, Asian tigers were struggling to survive, few decades later, they rose as Asian economic miracles astonishing the world with their economic development models, while Arabs were witnessing serious economic conditions.

Education is a prerequisite for democracy, and "if the revolution had a core, it was the young educated elite."[71] It is argued that education "promote[s] democracy both because it enables a 'culture of democracy' to develop and because it leads to greater prosperity, which is also thought to cause political development."[72] The most celebrated version of this argument is the modernization theory, popularized by Seymour Martin Lipset (1959), which emphasizes the role of education as well as economic growth in promoting political development in general and democracy in particular.

---

[71] Rander Pehrson and Justine Davis, *Germany And The Revolution of 1848-1849* (New York: Peter Lang, 1999), p. 145.

[72] Daron Acemoglu (2005), *op. cit.*, p. 44.

Lipset argues that education presumably broadens men's outlook, and enables them to understand the norms of tolerance. The better educated the population of a country the better chances for democracy"[73], and "if we cannot say that a 'high' level of education is a sufficient condition for democracy, the available evidence does suggest that it comes close to being a necessary condition."[74] Thus, "the uneducated man or the man with limited education is a different political actor from the man who has achieved a higher level of education."[75] We will borrow one of the tenets of the modernization theory, the education as a prerequisite for democracy. The modernization theory articulated a common view, which claims that high levels of schooling are both a prerequisite for democracy and a major cause of democratization.[76]

The relationship between education and democracy goes back to John Dewey who set an entire philosophy of

---

[73] Seymour Martin Lipset (1959), *op. cit.*, p. 79.

[74] *Ibid*, p. 80.

[75] Gabriel A. Almond and Sidney Verba, *The Civic Culture: Political Attitudes and Democracy in Five Nations* (London: Sage 1989), p. 315.

[76] Daron Acemoglu, Simon Johnson, James A. Robinson, and Pierre Yared (2005), *op. cit.*, p. 49.

democratic government, which has seen in increased education the spread of the basic requirement of democracy. Literacy, and education more generally, are of primary importance for democracy, but literacy seems to be more important as a foundation for democracy than any other aspect of modernization.[77] The role played by education is not simply to enable men to read and to comprehend the news. It is much more than providing literacy and training people to comprehend the issues of politics and to be effective political leaders and members of the bureaucracy. It helps to break down traditionalism, and to develop new attitudes and values such as openness to new experience and willingness to participate in civic affairs.[78]

The higher education is achieved the more likely to believe in democratic values and support democratic practices, and a better educated population of a country provides better chances for democracy to grow and sustain. The spread of education in Germany is linked to rejection of dictatorship in post Nazi era. If the level of

---

[77] James R. Pennock (1979), *op. cit.*, p. 59.

[78] Alex Inkeles (1969), *op. cit.*, p. 216.

education is not a sufficient condition for democracy, it comes lose to be a necessary condition in the modern world.[79]

The evidence on the contribution of education to democracy is more direct and strong in connection with individual behavior within countries. Data gathered by public opinion research agencies which have questioned people in different countries with their regard to their belief in various democratic norms of tolerance for opposition, to their attitude towards ethnic or racial minorities, and with regard to their belief in multi-party as against one-party systems have found that the most important single factor differentiating those giving democratic responses from others has been education.[80]

---

[79] James R. Pennock, *op. cit.*, p. 60.

[80] Seymour M. Lipset (1959), *op. cit.*, p. 81.

Chapter IV

Bahrain & Sudan: A Decisive Role of Education

The region remained immune to democracy since its independence in the aftermath of the World War II, while the world witnessed three waves of democratization. The stickiness to tyranny was due, in a part of it, to the blind support given to Arab authoritarian regimes by the Western powers. The region is witnessing a youth bulge, which makes it the second youngest region after Sub-Saharan Africa. This young society is also witnessing unprecedented levels of education that the region has accumulated throughout the last decades. A young and educated society was ready to rise up for democracy, better life conditions, and to change the political status quo. The self-immolation of Bouazizi was only the spark that ignited the events and drove people to the streets demanding freedom, dignity, and social justice.

The reason behind comparing educational attainments, through four education indicators in Bahrain and Sudan is to measure to what extent education is spread in the Arab and non-Arab Spring countries. Literacy, as the core of education, has a primary importance for democracy, because a literate society is a society aware of its rights and obligations and able to produce effective citizens. The role of literacy rates indicator is to measure the extent to which these two societies were literate, since literacy is the core of education, and education is the core of cultural and societal change towards democracy. Public spending on education is to measure the extent to which a country prioritizes education over other sectors in terms of its spending. Both as a percentage of Gross Domestic Product (GDP) and government expenditure, gives an indication of how a country prioritizes education in relation to its overall allocation of resources.

Gross enrollment rates indicator is to measure the spread of education among the population through four educational levels, pre-primary, primary, secondary, and tertiary level. It gives an idea about the percentage of the total number of students completing (or graduating from) the final year of primary or secondary, and tertiary education, regardless of age, expressed as a percentage of the population of the official graduation age. Finally gender parity indicator is to measure the extent to which women, in a given society, have equal access to education as men do. It gives an idea about women access to education, since women have played a pivotal role in the Arab Spring uprisings.

4.1. Overview of Bahrain & Sudan

Both Bahrain and Sudan have a long history of political authoritarianism since their independence, while in Sudan, series of putsches ended up with the tyrant regime of Omar Bashir who came to power through a coup d'état in 1989. Meanwhile, in Bahrain, political instability took place right after the independence, resulted an uprising in 1994, and political instability since 2001, and the outbreak of the Bahraini version of the Arab spring in 2011.

4.1.1. Bahrain: A Country Profile

The Khalifah family, a Sunni Muslim family member of the Bani Utbah tribe that expelled the Persians, has headed Bahrain since 1783. From 1861 to 1971 Bahrain was virtually a British protectorate. In Bahraini political system, the king, as the supreme authority, holds the main political and military posts with his ruling family members. In 1973, Emir Issa Ben Salman Ben Khalifa approved a constitution allowing elected parliament, where 74% were elected and around 26% were appointed. The parliamentary experiment came to a halt when the Emir dissolved parliament. An all-out campaign of arrests and torture followed, forcing many Bahraini intellectuals and activists to seek asylum in other countries, particularly in Europe. As the Iranian Revolution successfully toppled Shah's regime in 1979, Bahrain witnessed the emergence of religion-based political movements Sunni and Shia alike, but their major demands revolved around equality and a restoration of parliamentary life.[81]

Although the majority of Bahraini population is Shia, there is no accurate statistics about their percentage, and most of sources are unbiased, which varies from less than 57% to more 70%,[82] but it is likely to be around 60% of the population.[83] In 1994 an uprising led mainly, but not exclusively, by Shia parties finally culminated in the signing of the National Action Charter (NAC) in 2001, which was based on the restoration of parliamentary elections and political reforms. But in spite of two parliamentary elections, Hamad Ben Issa Al Khalifa, who succeeded his father and changed his title to king from emir (prince), which is a move supposedly aimed at

---

[81] Lamis Andoni, "Bahrain: Historical Struggle," http://www.aljazeera.com/indepth/opinion/2011/08/20118301473301296.html._(Search date: June 7, 2012)

[82] Scott Malcomson, "Bahrain: The Widening Gulf," http://6thfloor.blogs.nytimes.com/2011/03/16/bahrain-the-widening-gulf/. (Search date: July 5, 2012)

[83] "How Many Shia Are There In The World?" http://www.islamicweb.com/beliefs/cults/shiapopulatin.htm. (Search date: September 22, 2012)

establishing a constitutional monarchy, but he continued the regime's authoritarian and repressive policies.

The success of Jasmine Revolution in Tunisia and the Egyptian Revolution inspired Bahraini youth to pursue a new stage of their struggle. As early as February 2011, Bahraini youth were influenced by the winds of change blowing from the western part of the Arab World, Tunisia, Egypt, and Yemen. They staged protests and sit-ins demanding constitutional and political reforms. The organizers of the earlier protests were originally young people who did not necessarily belong to the predominantly Shia opposition parties. They did not rise as Shia but as youth who wanted to have a say on their fate through active political participation. The protests were peaceful and initially sought the implementation of 2001 NAC and an end of the security control over the country's political life. But as police forces started firing, demonstrators called for regime overthrow. The Saudi quickly intervened to restore the Sunni monarchy that faced the menace of a real revolution.

4.1.2. Sudan: A Country Profile

Before its independence in 1956, Sudan had been under the common governance of British-Egyptian condominium. In the aftermath of independence, it went under political instability, a period characterized by series of coup d'états and internal conflicts. Given that Sudan is a country where there is a clear difference predominantly Arab and Muslim north side and the predominantly African south, which has a population of mainly Christians and followers of indigenous religions. The country experienced its first putsch in 1958, followed by 1964 and 1969. The latter drove Jaafar Numairi to power as an ally to the Communist block; he escaped a coup d'état in 1971 with the help of the Army. In 1983, he shifted his ruling policy towards implying Sharia law. This policy shift displaced nearly two million and a long-standing civil war that ended up with the cession and the birth of Southern Sudan state in July 2011.

The war practically split the country in two; the larger northern part of Sudan remained under the official control of the Muslim pro-governmental army, and the

Sudan People's Liberation Army led by John Garang controlled the south and Silva Keer after him. But the division was unstable, by 1985, another coup removed Nimairi's regime from power. The new government was led by Sadiq al-Mahdi, an Oxford University graduate and an intellectual. However, he did not succeed in finding compromise with the rebelling south. In 1989, Omar Al-Bashir took power in Sudan through a military coup d'état and installed a one-party system led by the National Islamic Front (NIF). Al-Bashir became the official head of the state and the prime minister. The new regime was marked by a hard dictatorship, prohibition of any political activities that would not be in accordance with official propaganda, and suppression of any opposition.

Despite the long-standing dictatorship of Al-Bashir's regime, Sudan was far from being swept by early 2011 Arab Spring prodemocracy movements that toppled its neighboring stale regimes in Tunisia, Egypt, Libya, and Yemen. We will compare the spread of education among Bahraini and Sudanese population through four education indicators that were mentioned in the beginning of this chapter. Through which, we will explore the contribution of education in the outbreak of the Arab Spring.

4.2. Public Spending on Education

Human capital is an important determinant of economic growth and an effective vehicle for reducing inequality and absolute poverty. When countries invest in human capital through education, there is the potential for generating benefits to society that go beyond those acquired by the individuals who are involved. Not surprisingly, most developing countries, including the Arab countries, have committed substantial resources over the last 40 years to expand and improve their educational systems.[84] Public expenditure on education consists of current and capital public expenditure on education includes government spending on educational institutions (both public and private), education

[84] "The Road Not Traveled," *op. cit.*

administration as well as subsidies for private entities (students/ households and other privates entities).[85]

Public expenditure on education as a percentage of GDP gives an indication of how a country prioritizes education in relation to its overall allocation of resources. It includes spending on schools, universities and other public and private institutions involved in delivering or supporting educational services. At the tertiary level, spending on research and development can also be significant and is included in this indicator, to the extent that the research is performed by educational institutions. Public spending on education per student shows the expenditure on primary, secondary and tertiary education in relation to the number of students enrolled in each educational level. Public spending on education, as a percentage of total public spending, indicates the importance placed on education relative to that of other areas of public spending, such as health care, social security and national security.

---

[85] "Education Indicators: Technical guidelines," http://www.uis.unesco.org/Library/Documents/eguide9-en.pdf. (Search date: July 22, 2011)

4.2.1. Public Spending on Education in Bahrain

Bahrain is one of the leading Arab countries in achieving significant results of spreading education among its population. Usually the spread of education is the result of generous public spending on education. We will be discovering public spending as a percentage of GDP and as a percentage of government expenditure.

4.2.1.1. Total Public Spending on Education (as a percentage of government expenditure)

Public spending on education as a percentage of government expenditure is the total public education expenditure (current and capital) expressed as a percentage of total government expenditure in a given financial year. It includes government spending on educational institutions (both public and private), education administration and subsidies for private entities (students, households, and other private entities).[86] Table 4.1 shows that Bahrain's public spending

---

[86] "Education Indicators," *op. cit.*

on education as a percentage of government expenditure was 9.44% in 1980. This percentage rose four years later to 10.38% in 1984. The peak of this spending was in 2006 when Bahrain's expenditure reached 12.38%. Since then, slight increases and decreases occurred, 11.57% and 11.72% in 2007 and 2008 respectively. This percentage is high compared to the small number of the Bahraini population, which is less than a million.

Table 4.1: Public spending on education, total (% of government expenditure) 1980-2008

Year	Value
1980	9.44
1984	10.38
2006	12.83
2007	11.57
2008	11.72

Source: (UNESCO) Institute for Statistics

4.2.1.2. Total Public Spending on Education (as a percentage of GDP)

Total public expenditure on education as a percentage of GDP (current and capital) expressed as a percentage of the Gross Domestic Product (GDP) in a given financial year. This indicator shows the proportion of a country's wealth generated during a given financial year that has been spent by government authorities on education.[87] Table 4.2 indicates that Bahrain's public spending on education, as a percentage of GDP was 2.81% in 1980. The peak of spending on education was 3.76% in 1985. Since then, the spending decreased slightly and gradually to 3.35% and 3.03% in 2006 and 2007 respectively to reach its lowest level of 2.93% in 2008. These decreases might be because of the significant results that Bahrain registered by mid 2000s, when education was widely spread among the population.

The public spending on education is seen in the increasing numbers of pupils, schools (public and private), teachers, and students. Bahrain's educational system focuses on public schools, which explains high levels of government expenditure on education compared to consumer expenditure. This is led by a government program aimed at testing results in all areas of education (primary, secondary, and tertiary) and benchmarking these against international standards. This spending program, combined with a widespread lack of interest in private education by the majority, explains the much

---

[87] "Education Indicators," *op. cit.*

faster growth in government spending than in consumer spending and the much increasing educational attainment as a result.

Table 4.2: Public spending on education, total (% of GDP) 1980- 2008

Year	Value
1980	2.81
1985	3.76
2006	3.35
2007	3.03
2008	2.93

Source: (UNESCO) Institute for Statistics

Indeed Bahrain has registered tremendous gains in increasing the number of schools, classes, and students. In late 1970s, the number of schools in Bahrain was around 100; this number has increased to reach almost 2000 by early 2000s as shown in Table 4.3. The number of students almost doubled, and the number of teachers almost tripled in the same period. The number of teachers increased from 3557 in 1979 to 9667 in 2003, number of students moved from 67379 to 122356 in the same period of time in government education. Students in private education increased tremendously in almost a decade, increased from 12905 to 25792 early 2000s, in primary, secondary and tertiary education levels as indicates Table 5.4.

Table 4.3: Government Education
(Number of Students, Teachers, Classes and Schools) (1979-2004)

Academic Year	Schools		Classes		Teachers			Students		
	F	M	F	M	Total	F	M	Total	F	M
1979- 80	54	68	864	1045	3557	1735	1822	67379	30502	36877
1990-91	76	82	1498	1554	5834	2859	2975	100658	50055	50603
2000-01	95	98	1967	1936	7172	4332	2840	115818	59030	56788
2003-04	99	100	2115	2125	9667	5964	3803	122356	61816	60540

Source: Ministry of Education, Bahrain 2011

Table 5.4: Students in Private Schools By Level of Education and Sex - (1989- 2004)

Academic Year	Total			High Secondary		Secondary		Intermediate		Primary	
	Total	Female	Male	Female	Male	Female	Male	Female	Male	Female	Male
1989-90	12905	6094	6811	26	30	755	834	960	1020	4353	4927
2000-01	25128	11185	139443	389	429	1373	1617	2463	3202	6960	8695
2003-04	25792	11206	13986	34	38	1965	2297	2915	3620	8291	10366

Source: Ministry of Education, Bahrain 2011

Bahrain's spending on education was in a steady increase for the last three decades, despite the slight decrease in late 2000s. The results of this spending were seen through achieving a fully literate young society, and high gross enrollment rates. It is also seen through the increase of number of schools, classes, students, and the participation in education that made Bahrain among the pioneering Arab countries in achieving higher education levels among their population.

4.2.2. Public spending on education in Sudan

Bahrain had allocated significant resources to education as percentage of GDP and a percentage of government expenditure, while Sudan's allocation of its budget for both as a percentage of GDP and of government expenditure on education was very law through the last two decades.

4.2.2.1. Public spending on education, total (% of GDP)

The available data on education expenditures in Sudan is limited to the period of 1980-1996. This spending as a percentage of GDP shows considerable disparity and fluctuation in Sudan over this period. An imminent and continuous decline in public spending on education as a percentage of GDP occurred in 1985 as shown in Table 4.5. In 1980, Sudan spent 4.8% of its GDP on education in 1980. The lowest spending on education was 0.6% in 1991 (under Bashir's rule), and a slight increase occurred in

1996, when the spending was 1.4% of the GDP. We suppose that expenditure on education continued its decline because the spending on education as a percentage of government expenditure was in a significant decline from 1986 towards 2002.

Table 4.5: Public spending on education, total (% of GDP) 1980 - 1996

Year	Value
1980	4.8
1985	4
1990	0.9
1991	0.6
1996	1.4

Source: (UNESCO) Institute for Statistics 2011

4.2.2.2. Public spending on education, total (as a percentage of government expenditure)

In addition to the obvious and continuous decline on spending on education as a percentage of GDP, public spending on education as a percentage of total government expenditure also witnessed a sharp decline. Table 4.6, shows that over the period of 1986-2002, spending on education in Sudan was in a sharp and continuous decline from 15.1% in 1986 to 6.9% in 2002. Government spending on education in Sudan reached its lowest levels of 2.8% in 1990. A certain increase occurred from 1998, but it is still very low compared to the number of Sudanese population, which is one of the highest in the Arab world.

Table 4.6: Public spending on education, total (% of government expenditure) 1986-2002

Year	Value
1986	15.1
1990	2.8
1998	4.8
1999	7.7
2000	7
2001	6.4
2002	6.9

Source: (UNESCO) Institute for Statistics 2011

In Sudan, the extent of privatization shows an increasing trend in tertiary education faster than in secondary and basic education respectively. Until 1990, tertiary education was publicly provided, and there were only two private universities compared to 17 public higher education institutions and universities. The number of private tertiary education institutions increased from two in 1990 to 26 in 2000. The share of private tertiary education institutions increased from 11% in 1990 to 50% in 2000 to be equivalent to the share of public tertiary education institutions, in 2008/2009. But the share of private 52% is larger than the share of public 48% in total higher education institutions in Sudan. However, the increasing private investment on education should not hide the fact that educational investment is almost entirely dependent on the public sector, with a very minimal contribution from private sector in Sudan.[88]

The comparison of public spending on education between Bahrain and Sudan shows that Bahrain spent more on education than Sudan did. In Bahrain public spending as a percentage of government expenditure was 9.44% in 1980 and increased to reach its peak of 12.83% in 2006 with a slight decline to 11.72% in 2008. Generally, an important increase was seen over time, regardless of its slight increases and decreases. For Sudan, public spending started with 15.1% in 1986, and dropped to 6.9% in 2002. Generally Sudan's spending was in decrease and

---

[88] Samia Satti Osman Mohamed Nour, "Education, Training And Skill Development Policies In Sudan: Macro and Micro Overview," http://www.merit.unu.edu/publications/wppdf/2011/wp2011-032.pdf. (Search date: February 13, 2012)

less than its comparator example of Bahrain. The same results were achieved in public spending as a percentage of GDP. Sudan started with higher percentage of 4.8% in 1980, and decreased to 1.4% in 1996, meanwhile, Bahrain increased, even slightly, its expenditure as a percentage of GDP from 2.81% to 2.93% in 2008.

4.3. Literacy Rates

Choosing literacy rate as an indicator to measure the spread of education is because of its importance as a foundation for democracy, and as the core of education. We borrowed the definition adopted by The United Nations Educational, Scientific and Cultural Organization (UNESCO) in 1978, which defines "a person [who] is functionally literate [is the person] who can engage in all those activities in which literacy is required for effective functioning of his group and community and also for enabling him to continue to use reading, writing and calculation for his own and the community's development."[89] In this definition, "literacy refers to a context-bound continuum of reading, writing and numeracy skills, acquired and developed through processes of learning and application, in schools and in other settings appropriate to youth and adults."[90]

Literacy strengthens the capabilities of individuals, families and communities to access health, educational, political, economic and cultural opportunities and services. Literacy is not only about reading and writing, but it goes beyond that to train effective citizens to be able to comprehend issues of politics. Since the Arab Spring was youth-driven prodemocracy movement, the emphasis will be on youth literacy (15-24), without disregarding the role of adult literacy too.

4.3.1. Literacy Rates in Bahrain

Bahrain has registered tremendous gains in combating illiteracy among its population in the last two decades. In

---

89 "Education Indicators: Technical guidelines," *op. cit.*

90 "Education for All: Literacy For Life," http://www.uis.unesco.org/Library/Documents/gmr06-en.pdf. (Search date: July 25, 2011)

terms of youth literacy (15-24), Bahrain is the first Arab country to achieve a fully literate young society. As table 4.6 indicates, literacy rate among youth (15-24) rose from 96.9% in 1991 to 100% in 2009, while the Arab regional average was 87.9%. Youth literacy rates among male and females rose from 97.3% and 96.6% respectively in 1991 to a fully literate young society (100%) in 2009. By 2009, Bahrain became the first Arab country to fully eradicate illiteracy among its youth.

Tremendous efforts were also done to increase literacy among adults (15 years and above). Table 4.6 shows that adult literacy rate among adult was 84% in 1991 with 88.5% and 76.9% among males and females were respectively, while the Arab regional average of 2009 was 72.7%. This percentage reached 91.4% by 2009, with 90.2% and 92.2% among females and males respectively. Although these results are lower than other parts of the world, but the notable progress and significant efforts made Bahrain a pioneering Arab country.

The percentage of illiteracy among the Bahraini population dropped dramatically in a decade from 1991 census to 2001. This ratio amounted to 7.5% for males and

17% for females and 12.3% for the two types together in 2001. While the illiteracy rate in the corresponding 1991 amounted to 13.3% for males and 28.7% for females and 21.0% for the two together.[91]

Table 4.6: Literacy Rates Among Youth and Adult in Bahrain (%) 1991-2009

Literacy rates		1991	2009	2009 Regional Average
Adult (15+)	MF	84.0	91,4	72.7
	M	88.5	92,2	81.4
	F	76.9	90.2	63.5
Youth (15-24)	MF	96.9	100.0	87.9
	M	97.3	100.0	91.3
	F	96.6	100.0	84.4

Source: UNESCO - UIS 2011

4.3.2. Literacy Rates in Sudan

Sudan made significant progress in increasing literacy rates among its youth (15-24) which rose from 78.2% in 2000 to 85,9% in 2009, as shown in Table 4.7; a progress that is still below the Arab regional average of 2009 (87.9%). Both literacy among males (89.1%) and females (82.7%) are below the Arab regional averages (91.3%) and

91 "Kingdom of Bahrain: General Profile," http://www.unesco.org/fileadmin/MULTIMEDIA/INSTITUTES/UIL/confintea/pdf/National_Reports/Arab%20States/Bahrain.pdf. (Search date: September 13, 2012)

(84.4%) respectively. Literacy rates among adults (15+) rose from 61.3% in 2000 to 70.2% in 2009, which is still below the Arab regional average at 72.7%.

Unlike Bahrain, Sudan's achievements in spreading literacy among its population were very low. Despite the progress that was done through the last decade by increasing youth literacy rates from 78.2% in 2000 to 85.7% in 2009, this rate is still below the Arab regional average of 2009. Meanwhile, Bahrain has achieved a fully literate young society by reaching 100% for both males and females as the first Arab country to eradicate illiteracy among its youth. Bahrain also registered impressive results in spreading literacy among adult population; adult literacy rate reached 91.4% in 2009. Through the comparison of the first indicator, Bahrain is ahead of Sudan in terms of spreading literacy, as the core of education, among its population, while Sudan is still lagging behind.

Table 4.7: Literacy Rates Among Youth and Adult in Sudan (%) 1991-2009

Literacy rates		2000	2009	2009 Regional Average
Adult (15+)	MF	61.3	70.2	72.7
	M	67.2	79.6	81.4
	F	43.6	60.8	63.5
Youth (15-24)	MF	78.2	85.9	87.9
	M	85.7	89.1	91.3
	F	72.3	82.7	84.4

Source: UNESCO - UIS 2011

Bahrain, as an Arab Spring country, has achieved relatively very high literacy rates among its adult population, and a fully literate young society. While it reached 96.0% of youth literacy rates in 1991, Sudan hardly registered 78.2% a decade later, in 2000. By 2009, Bahrain reached fully literate young society; Sudan's youth literacy rate was still below the Arab regional average of 2009. Jordan was the first Arab country to take to the streets when Tunisians succeeded in driving their president out of the country. Like Tunisia and Bahrain, it has registered significant progress in spreading literacy among its young as well as adult population, and bridging the educational gender gap. Youth literacy reached 98.9% in 2007, male literacy was 99% and female was 98.9%. The gap between male and females is very close almost 0.1%. In terms of adult literacy, tremendous results were also achieved 92.2%, where male literacy reached 95.5% and female literacy 88.9%. But the educational gender gap is still wide compared with Bahrain.

4.4. Gross Enrollment Rates

Gross Enrollment Rates (GER) is defined as the total number of students completing (or graduating from) the final year of primary or secondary education, regardless of age, expressed as a percentage of the population of the official primary or secondary graduation age.[92] We chose GER instead of Net Enrollment Rate (NER), because GER is used as a substitute indicator to NER when data on enrollment by single years of age are not available. It can also be a complementary indicator to NER by indicating the extent of over-aged and under-aged enrolment.

---

92 "Education Indicators: Technical guidelines," *op. cit.*

4.4.1. Gross Enrollment Rates in Bahrain

We will measure education attainment in Bahrain through gross enrollment rates in four levels of education, from pre-primary to tertiary education. As mentioned above GER is giving the total number of students regardless of age in a given level of education, expressed as a percentage of education.

4.4.1.1. Pre-Primary Enrollment

The period of 1991-2002 witnessed important changes in the number of children enrolled in pre-primary education level. The total registration rate was 38% in 1998 compared with 25% in 1991, as shown in Table 4.8. This tremendous increase is an evident proof that illustrates the growing educated society of Bahrain and the interest of the Bahrain to reach a fully educated society starting with the pre-primary education. Bahrain's GER in the pre-primary education of 1991 (25%) was above the Arab regional average of 2009 (21%) as shown in Table 4.8. This is another sign that Bahrain is a pioneering country in spreading education and seeking a fully educated society.

Table 4.8: Gross Enrollment Rate in the Pre-primary Education (%) 1991-2009

Pre-primary		1991	1999	2002	2009	2009 Regional Average
GER %	MF	25	38	42	NA	21
	M	25	39	44	NA	21
	F	25	37	41	NA	20

Source: UNESCO - UIS 2011

However, enrollment opportunities in kindergartens are available for both genders without exception but enrolment depend mainly on the family financial situation, in addition to the family awareness of the importance of this stage in preparing children for primary education. It is evident that all children who have attended kindergartens programs and have reached official primary education age (6 years) enroll in public or private schools. An important increase has occurred in the 1990s in the number of primary education children who attended early childhood programs.

4.4.1.2. Primary Education Enrollment rate:

This indicator demonstrates the number of students enrolled in primary education as a percentage of the estimated size of population in the same age group. The percentage of literate youth reached 100% in Bahrain among both males and females alike. In this sense, Bahrain has made available primary education to all children. Table 4.9 shows that the Arab regional average of 2009, which was 97%, Bahrain exceeded it in 1991 when GER among males reached 113% and 112% among females. Even this percentage witnessed a slight decline a decade later down to 111% in 2002, but it is still above the Arab regional average. Despite the unavailability of 2009 data, we believe that Bahrain continued its steady progress and would have reached higher results, comparing this indicator with literacy indicator, which reached 100% by 2009.

Table 4.9: Gross Enrollment Rate in the Primary Education (%) 1991-2009

Primary		1991	1999	2002	2009	2009 Regional Average
GER %	MF	112	107	111	NA	97
	M	112	107	113	NA	101
	F	113	107	109	NA	93

Source: UNESCO - UIS 2011

4.4.1.3. Secondary Education Enrollment rate

Secondary enrollment is the total enrollment in secondary education as a proportion of the population of secondary school age according to national regulations. This indicator is used in monitoring the general status and trends of participation, and assesses the relation between demand and supply of educational opportunities. Taking the same period as pre-primary and primary gross enrollment rate, Bahrain's results of early 1990s were much above the Arab regional average. Bahrain reached 101% in 1990, while the Arab regional average of 2009 was 68%, despite the slight decrease of GER in 2002 and despite the unavailability of 2009 data as shown in Table 4.10.

Table 4.10: Gross Enrollment Rate in the Secondary Education (%) 1991-2009

Secondary		1991	1999	2002	2009	2009 Regional Average
GER %	MF	101	96	99	NA	68
	M	98	92	95	NA	71
	F	103	101	103	NA	65

Source: UNESCO - UIS 2011.

4.4.1.4. Tertiary Education Enrollment Rate

Bahrain's achievements in tertiary education in 1999 were almost as high as the Arab regional average of 2009.

The GER in tertiary education in 1999 was 21% while the Arab regional average of 2009 was 22%. In this level of education, the gender gap was bigger in favor of females since 1991, because tertiary enrollment among females was 20% while 15% among males. A decade later, this rate rose only by 1% among males (16%), while among females it reached 28%, which was higher than the 2009 Arab regional average of 22% as indicates Table 4.11.

Table 4.11: Gross Enrollment Rate in the Tertiary Education (%) 1991-2009

Tertiary		1991	1999	2002	2009	2009 Regional Average
GER %	MF	17	21	NA	NA	22
	M	15	16	NA	NA	23
	F	20	28	NA	NA	22

Source: UNESCO - UIS 2011

Bahrain's gross enrollment rates' achievements in pre-primary, primary and secondary levels were significant. Bahrain was two decades ahead of the Arab regional average; meanwhile the tertiary gross enrollment rate of 1999 was as almost as the Arab regional average of 2009. Therefore, Bahrain as an Arab Spring country was a pioneering country in spreading education, because the pupils of pre-primary, primary, and even secondary in 1990s and early 2000s are the generation that took to the streets early 2011 demanding freedom and democracy. The spectacular results of GER in all the levels achieved in Bahrain were not the same in the case of Sudan.

4.4.2. Gross Enrollment Rates in Sudan

Through this paragraph we will measure the GER in Sudan in all levels of education, in pre-primary, primary, secondary, and tertiary education, the same way it was compared in the case of Bahrain.

4.4.2.1. Pre-Primary Enrollment

Over the last decade Sudan has made a certain progress in spreading education through pre-primary enrollment level among its population. Pre-primary enrollment was 27% in 2009, which was above the Arab regional average of 2009 (21%). During the first decade (1991-99) there was a slight decline from 18% to 17%, but the main achievement was in the last decade, where it rose to 27% as shown in table 4.12. This significant progress might be the result of the pressure exercised by international institutions and donors to prioritize education in its national strategies, as well as people's awareness of the importance of education. Generally, Sudan made a progress in spreading education among its population in terms of pre-primary education level, but considering the size of its population and its late efforts, it is still lagging behind its comparator case of Bahrain.

Table 4.12: Gross Enrollment Rate in the Pre-Primary Education (%) 1991-2009

Pre-primary		1991	1999	2002	2009	2009 Regional Average
GER %	MF	18	19	17	27	21
	M	22	NA	17	26	21
	F	13	NA	17	27	20

Source: UNESCO - UIS 2011

4.4.2.2. Primary Enrollment

Sudan has made modest progress in primary enrollment throughout the period of 1991-2005, where there was only a slight progress from 48% to 52%, but through the last decade a significant improvement was done. Overall, Sudan's efforts were still very modest despite the big jump from 52% in 2002 to 73% in 2009 it is still below the Arab regional average of 2009 (97%). This progress is the results of Sudan's late efforts to improve education among its population. A quick look at GER among males and females shows that in 1991, it was 54% and 42% and rose to 76% and 69% among males and females respectively, as shown in Table 4.13.

Table 4.13: Gross Enrollment Rate in the Primary Education (%) 1991-2009

Primary		1991	1999	2002	2009	2009 Regional Average
GER %	MF	48	48	52	73	97
	M	54	52	56	76	101
	F	42	44	47	69	93

Source: UNESCO - UIS 2011

4.4.2.3. Secondary Enrollment

By early 1990s, Sudan's GER in secondary enrollment was very modest. It registered 21% in 1991, with 23% and 18% for males and females respectively. Despite the notable progress during the past two decades where the GER in secondary education was almost doubled from 21% to 39%, GER was barely half of the Arab regional average of 2009 (68%) as shown in Table 4.14.

Table 4.14: Gross Enrollment Rate in the Secondary Education (%) 1991-2009

Secondary		1991	1999	2002	2009	2009 Regional Average
GER %	MF	21	26	29	39	68
	M	23	NA	30	41	71
	F	18	NA	28	36	65

Source: UNESCO - UIS 2011

4.4.2.4. Tertiary Enrollment

Despite the scarcity of data on tertiary enrollment in Sudan, it is obvious that attainment was very low, compared to the previous results accumulated in the previous levels of attainment, the size of the population, and the free educational system. Moreover, registering 6% in 1999 is low compared to Bahrain's achievement in the same year, as shown in Table 4.15. Although no available data for the last decade, we may presume that no significant progress was registered due to low attainment in the previous levels in the last decade and the low spending in education as well.

Table 4.15: Gross Enrollment Rate in the Tertiary Education (%) 1991-2009

Tertiary		1991	1999	2002	2009	2009 Regional Average
GER %	MF	NA	6	NA	NA	22
	M	NA	6	NA	NA	23
	F	NA	6	NA	NA	22

Source: UNESCO - UIS 2011

Bahrain has accumulated impressive results in spreading education among its population, while Sudan's achievements were very modest. The wide gap can be seen through the four levels of attainment from pre-primary to tertiary education. The impressive results of Bahrain through the four levels of attainment were 27% (2009), 11% (2002), 99% (2002), and 21% (2002), while Sudan's were 27% (2009), 73% (2009), 39 (2009), and 6% (1999) in pre-primary, primary, secondary, and tertiary enrollment respectively. Despite the modest results of Sudan in the last decade there was a significant progress for both pre-primary and primary enrollment. The new shift in Sudan's policy will surely produce an educated generation, if they survive their educational attainment till the tertiary level, they might ignite and fuel the second wave of the Arab Spring.

4.5. Gender Parity in Education

Gender issues can be considered with reference to different kinds of data sets. At the simplest level one can consider the absolute figures and the absolute difference between the numbers of male and female illiterates, pupils, students, teachers, etc. Similar considerations can be applied to derived statistics in the form of indicators such as literacy rates, admission rates, enrolment ratios, school survival and so on.[93] We will use the gender parity in its simplest level, since it is concerned with the access of females to education compared to males. The gender parity has three dimensions, educational (ratio of females to males in various stages of education), economic (women's share in paid work outside the agricultural sector), and political dimension (women's share of parliamentary seats). We will focus only on the educational dimension to measure the spread of education, since this essay is trying to test the role of education in the outbreak of the Arab Spring uprisings in 2011.

4.5.1. Gender Parity in Education in Bahrain

Generally, Bahrain has succeeded in achieving the elimination of disparities in all stages of education, where available data indicates that the ratio of females to males

---

93 "Gender-Sensitive Education Statistics And Indicators A Practical Guide," http://www.uis.unesco.org/Education/Documents/unesco-gender-sensitive-edstats-indicators.pdf. (Search date: March 11, 2012)

in various stages of education start as converging at the primary level, then become in favor of females in the other stages (intermediate, secondary, and university). For literacy among youth, Bahrain was successful in eliminating the disparities, while among adults significant efforts were done to bridge the gap. These ratios have been stable in Bahrain since the early 1990s. We will measure gender parity in education through literacy rates and gross enrollment rates.

4.5.1.1. Literacy Rate among Males and Females

Throughout the last two decades (1991-2009), Bahrain has made significant progress in bridging the gap between males and females. By 2009, it was able to fully literate its youth, where the gap between males and females was zero among youth (15-24). Bahrain was the first and the only Arab country to bridge the gender parity gap in literacy early 1990s among youth. In 1994, the gender parity in youth literacy was slightly in favor of males 97.3% than females 96.6%, but the gap was higher in adult literacy in favor of men with 88.5% to 76.9% among women. The outcome of the tremendous efforts during the last two decades was to eliminate the gap in youth literacy and reduce it to 1.8% in favor of males in adult literacy with 92% among males and 90.2% among females. Rapid and significant progress put Bahrain on the right track to be the first Arab country to eradicate gender gap among youth and reduce it to very low levels among adults.

4.5.1.2. The Ratio of Females to Males in All Stages of Education from Pre-primary to Tertiary Levels

There is a closer female to male ratio to one during the primary stage, but it rises in the intermediate and secondary levels in general, and it is more than one in favor of females in the total three phases, which means that the goal of gender parity was achieved in mid 1990s. In pre-primary education, gender parity was zero, with 25% for both males and females. In primary level, it was 1% in favor of females (113% to 112%), although this percentage shifted in favor of males by 2002 in both levels. In secondary and tertiary levels, since 1990s it was in favor of females. In 1990s, the gender parity was in favor of females with 103% and 20% in secondary and tertiary attainments, while among men 98% and 15% in both levels of attainments. A decade later, the gender parity was still in favor of females.

As for tertiary level, there are 1.6 times more females than males in higher education in 2005 in all universities. In the University of Bahrain the number of females exceeded by 2.2 times that of males, in the Gulf University by about 3 times, and in the Faculty of Health Sciences by 5.4 times. The Bahrain Training Institute constituted the exception, with around 2.1 times more males than females. This means that the goal of gender equality between men and women is also achieved at the level of university education.[94]

4.5.2. Gender Parity in Education in Sudan

Sudan's performance falls below the developing countries and the Arab world level in terms of adult literacy, youth literacy, gross primary enrolment, gross

---

[94] "Towards Achieving the Millennium Development Goals: Progress of Work (2004-2007)," http:// www.undp.org.bh/Files/2008MDGPROREP/Introduction BHR-MDG-PROREP.pdf. (Search date: July 23, 2012)

secondary enrolment, female economic activity rate (percentage ages 15 and above and percentage of male rate ages 15 and above). Moreover, Sudan's performance in terms of female/ male rate in adult literacy rate, gross primary enrolment and female economic activity rate falls also below the Arab countries, Sub Saharan Africa, low income and least developed countries. Moreover, Sudan not only lagging behind in terms of rank and performance, but also there was no remarkable progress shown over time.[95]

4.5.2.1. Literacy Rate among Males and Females

The statistics of literacy among youth and adult in Sudan show that the gap between males and females is high compared with Bahrain. In 2009, literacy among youth was 89.1% and 82.7% among males and females respectively, which shows that the gap in adult literacy is higher than youth literacy. In 2009, literacy among men was 79%, and 60.8% among females. Very modest results

---

[95] Samia Satti Osman Mohamed Nour, "Assessment of The State of Women and Gender Gap in Sudan," http://www.arab-api.org/conf_0310/p27.pdf. (Search date: July 23, 2012)

compared with Bahrain in the same period. In general, Sudan's performance in literacy is lagging behind many Arab countries and some Sub-Saharan least developed countries.

4.5.2.2. The Ratio of Females to Males in All Levels of Education from Pre-primary to Tertiary

In general, Sudan has registered low educational attainment results compared with Arab or Sub-Saharan countries. Despite the achievements in pre-primary and primary enrollment, Sudan was lagging behind Bahrain. In the educational attainment, the gap between women and men's current access to education is captured through ratios of women to men in primary, secondary, and tertiary level of education. A longer-term view of the country's ability to educate women and men in equal numbers is captured through the ratio of the female literacy rate to the male literacy rate.[96]

Through the statistics of gross enrollment rates in pre-primary, primary, secondary, and tertiary education, the

---

[96] Samia Satti, *op. cit.*

gap between the enrolled genders is high. In pre-primary education, the parity gap was 22% to 13% in favor of females early 1990s; this rate shifted in favor of females (27% to 26%) two decades later. In primary education, enrollment rate was in favor of males in 1991, 55% and 42% for males and females respectively, and remained in favor of males two decades later (56% to 47%) in 2009. In 1991, enrollment rate was 23% and 18% among males and females respectively, and remained in favor of males with 41% to 36% two decades later.

In terms of literacy rates, has achieved relatively high literacy rates among its adult population, and a fully literate young society. While Bahrain reached 96.0% of youth literacy rates in 1991, Sudan barely registered 78.2% a decade later. By 2009, Bahrain reached 91.4% of literate adult society, while Sudan's results (70.2%) were below Arab regional average (72.7%).

In terms of gross enrollment rates, Bahrain was ahead of Sudan. In pre-primary education, its enrollment rate was 42% in 2002, while in Sudan it was 27% in 2009. In terms of primary education, Bahrain's GER was 111% in 2002, while 73% for Sudan in 2009. In secondary and tertiary education, Sudan's results were very modest, compared with the Arab regional average 68% and 22% for both levels respectively, which were 39% and 6% for secondary and tertiary education respectively. Bahrain's GER's was 99% in 2002 for secondary education, which was much above the Arab regional average of 2009. For tertiary education, Bahrain registered 21% in 2002, which was almost as high as the Arab regional average of 2009.

In terms of public spending on education, the comparison shows that Bahrain spent more on education than Sudan did. Public spending as a percentage of government expenditure in Bahrain was 9.44% of its budget in 1980, and it reached its peak in 2006 with 12.83% to witness a slight decline to 11.72% in 2008. Sudan's spending started as high as 15.1% in 1986 to drop down to 6.9% in 2002. The same results were achieved in public spending as a percentage of GDP. Sudan started with higher percentage 4.8% in 1980, to drop down to 1.4% in 1996, while Bahrain started with 2.81% to end up with 2.93% in 2008.

In addition to the low enrollment rates in all levels of education, the gap between the enrolled genders is high.

In pre-primary, male enrollment was 22% and 13% for females early 1990s; this rate witnessed an increase in favor of females, which registered 27% while 26% for males in 2009. In primary education, enrollment rate was in favor of males in 1991, 55% and 42% for males and females respectively, two decades later, males still ahead of females with 56% and 47% in 2009. Same results were registered in secondary enrollment, the very low enrollment rate results low gap too. In 1991, enrollment rate was 23% and 18% among males and females respectively, two decades later, still in favor of males with 41% and 36% for females.

As the literature of the relationship between democracy and education indicates that there is a high correlation between education and democracy. Through the comparative cases of Bahrain and Sudan, we found out that Bahrain has achieved higher educational attainment levels, while Sudan accumulated very low levels. The role of education is to broaden men's minds, enable them to understand their own political issues, and to become effective citizens. Countries with higher levels of education are more likely both to experience a transition from dictatorship to democracy, and to withstand anti-democratic challenges. Moreover, the size of the most successful challenger regime to an existing dictatorship rises with the level of education. Huntington pointed out that education is a powerful predictor of permanent transitions from dictatorship to democracy.[97]

Bahrain had a steady increase in educational attainment; it was the first Arab country to reach a fully literate young society, and high levels of literacy among adults compared to other Arab countries. In early 1990s, when most of Arab countries were struggling to combat illiteracy among their youth, Bahrain was ahead for both youth and adult literacy as well as educational attainments from primary to tertiary levels. In 1994, an uprising took place in Bahrain demanding political change and freedom, and the establishment of the rule of law. Bahrain was the only country among Gulf Cooperation Council countries to witness an uprising for democracy and political reform, with the rise of an active civil society.

---

97 - S. Huntington, Democracy's Third Wave, Journal of Democracy, Vol 2, N 2, Spring 1991.

Historically, media tools that exist in any given time or society were to be used to spread ideas, and to communicate mostly when there is a tight control of governments on public social media. During the French Revolution printing machines were used to transmit ideas and to galvanize people, and the same role audiocassette tapes played an imminent role during the Iranian Revolution. The Internet is one of the most important developments in communication technology in our time; it breaks the monopoly of communication that was previously confined to governments and political parties. It empowers individuals to become political broadcasters and voice their opinions on an equal footing with any other user. Communication is characterized by informality, which may in turn encourage further freedom of expression. Moreover the Internet creates an area that is difficult for the government or other entities to control, which is an important advantage in states where media are centrally controlled.

Educated youth used Internet as a tool to spread their ideas and to galvanize people to rise up against authoritarian regimes. In a study conducted by New York

Institute of Technology about Bahraini blogs analyzed the existing of Bahraini blogs that were at the center of the exchange of political ideas and found a total number of roughly 150 blogs in 2010, which existed since 2001.[98] "Political blog means a blog that devotes a large part of its comments to politics. 27 % of the 150 blogs examined, would qualify as political, 65% of the 150 bloggers use mainly in English, which means only educated people can have write and understand. Although each blog has a specific character, authors share many observations in the area of political developments. The main subjects that appear simultaneously in most blogs include assessment of members of parliament, criticism of policies and protests against Internet censorship."[99]

Bahraini bloggers enthusiastically followed developments in the political scene. They criticized the overwhelming focus of parliament members on moral issues, rather than on providing realistic solutions, and for restraining

---

98 Magdalena Maria Karolak, "Civil Society and Web 2.0 Technology: A Study of Social Media in The Kingdom of Bahrain," http://www.arabmediasociety.com/articles/downloads/20110531112812_Karolak.pdf. (Search date: December 21, 2012)

99 *Ibid.*

freedom. "The years 2008 and 2009 witnessed a number of proposals aimed at preserving the religious identity of the country, such as a complete ban on pork, alcohol in public places, entertainment in hotels, and concerts. The incompetence of parliamentarians made bloggers conclude that the core problem lies within voters themselves, who elected the parliament members and are responsible for the choices made some bloggers reflected further on the state of Bahraini society and were critical of animosities and the lack of political education. Demonstrations under the name of democracy took place in 2007."[100]

Educated women in Bahrain discussed their own issues, through Internet, such as the bitter disputes in parliament about family law, and other issues of primary importance to them. They are also working on the ground through many civil organizations. Non-governmental associations such as the Bahrain Businesswomen's Society, Bahrain Women's Association for Human Development, and

---

[100] Luke Schleusener, "From Blog to street: The Bahraini public sphere in transition," http://www.arabmediasociety.com/?article=15. (Search date: December 21, 2012)

Bahrain Women's Association to promote gender equality and the protection from unjust treatment and abuse. Women's associations have become more and more vocal on the political scene, demanding the reform of women's status in society. Human rights associations, including the Migrant Workers Protection Society, also operate successfully in Bahrain. Most of these activities are part of the daily political life issues where educated women participate and give their opinion as a way to promote democracy in their country.[101]

Bahraini youth used social network platforms in gathering supporters, organizing the movement as well as coordinating protests. Anti-government sentiment had been fermenting in Bahrain for the past three decades, leading occasionally to violent upheavals. The protests intensified throughout the 2000s. In 2005 and in 2008 Bahrain was shaken by demonstrations based on economic and political demands. The opposition planned nationwide protests during the Formula 1 race in May 2009, an international event with international visitors from all over the world, which would have international

---

101 Magdalena M. Karolak, *op. cit.*

impacts. The accomplishments of the Tunisian and Egyptian revolutions provided an opportunity to bring international sympathy and attention on Bahrain. Thus Bahraini activists organized themselves on Facebook, promoting the idea of a national 'Day of Rage'. They called on all their followers to take to the streets and organize an Egyptian-style occupation of Bahrain's largest square. This essay may conclude that the role of education in the outbreak of the Bahraini Arab Spring uprising was pivotal, because Bahrain has successfully spread education among its population; meanwhile Sudan was still lagging behind, which we may conclude it was the main reason it did not join the Arab Spring club early 2011.

• Chapter V •

Conclusion

For the first time in recent Arab history, millions of Arabs poured to the streets in unprecedented, simultaneous, and spontaneous waves from Morocco to Syria shouting the same slogans: 'freedom, dignity, and justice'. In the eve of the outbreak of these uprisings, the Arab region was witnessing the rise of a new generation of Arab tyrants preparing to inherit power in what is constitutionally called "Republics" in Tunisia, Yemen, Egypt, and Libya in an attempt to duplicate the North Korean and Syrian models. High unemployment rates, mainly among university graduates, wounded dignity from series of humiliations, and a young boiling educated society seeking a better future. A small event, which nobody would have expected its impact and consequences, has changed the realities on the ground and reshaped the fate of millions of people across the region. The self-immolation act of a desperate street vendor has ignited series of popular uprisings, which was the worst nightmare of the "beloved" Arab leaders in the eve of the new year of 2011.

Education had a pivotal contribution in the outbreak of the Arab spring uprisings. As the focus is on the spread of education mainly among youth as a pivotal factor in the outbreak of the Arab Spring prodemocracy movements. This essay aims to analyze the role of education in the outbreak of the Arab Spring uprisings early 2011, regardless of their failure or success in changing in the structure of the tyrant regimes.

The analysis of cases of Bahrain and Sudan confirm the hypothesis that education has a pivotal contribution in the outbreak of the Arab Spring. Four education indicators were selected to measure the spread of education in these countries: literacy rates, spending on education, gross enrollment rates, and gender parity in education. We found out that Arab Spring countries have higher education levels among its population, while non-Arab Spring countries have lower levels. The case of Bahrain suggests how the spread of education has contributed to the outbreak of the Arab Spring, while the case of Sudan shows how the lack of education is the reason why Sudan did not join the Arab Spring club.

As one might question the ability of education to trigger uprisings in any country, we argue that education is the fundamental cause that facilitated the way to this astonishing change in the Arab world. The region witnessed series of uprisings in the post-independence era in Egypt 1977, 1984, 2008; Morocco, 1981, 1984, 1990; Tunisia, 1984, 2008; and Algeria 1985,1988, etc., but their influence and momentum was very limited. The spread of education among Arab population was much lower than the levels that were accumulated late 2000s. The role of education can be seen in the Arab streets when Arab youth organized themselves, having clear perception in their minds that changing the regimes is the cure for the 'diseases' of the region. They benefitted from the opportunities that Internet and social media brought along. Moreover, literature argues that education is an important condition and a pre-requisite for planting democracy in any given society.

For many decades, the Arab region remained as the largest area immune to democracy while the world was experiencing multiple democratization waves, the last one only a few miles away from the Arab shores. Since the aim of this essay is to understand the causes and circumstances that led to the sudden outbreak of the Arab Spring, and the causes that made the Arab region immune to democracy. We found out that the spread of education was pivotal for the successful Arab uprisings of 2011, and the lack of education was behind the failure of the previous Arab uprisings.

Education is the fundamental factor that triggered the events and this essay does not deny the role of other factors in igniting the first spark that easily galvanized people to take to the streets. However, education brought cultural and mental change to the area. Therefore, Arabs, mainly youth, became aware that the failures of the area to achieve economic development, defend the Arab main issues, humiliate Arab people is rooted in the stale regimes. In early 1960s, the 'Asian tigers' were struggling to survive, and few decades later; they rose as Asian economic miracles astonishing the world with their economic development models.

Internet and social media played a facilitating role, providing information, fast communication, and coordination among activists. In the French Revolution, prints played a role in spreading the revolutionary ideas; radio tapes were important in circulating the idea of the Iranian revolution. In the early 2000s, cell phone text messages and emails played a pivotal role in spreading information among activists in Serbia, who finally succeeded in overthrowing Milosevic's regime. Since the Iranian students' movement in 2009, the role of Twitter and Facebook as tools in galvanizing people to the streets increased, but revolutions cannot be twitted and cannot be launched behind computer screens. Social media only facilitated and speeded up the events on the way to social and political changes.

As discussed in the theoretical part, since regime change literature suggests that education is a precondition for the planting of democracy and its consolidation, this essay raises the question: to what extent will democracy be sustained and consolidated in post-revolution Arab Spring countries? It is necessary to take in consideration the facts that education has reached unprecedented levels in these societies and also political Islam is playing an important role, which might be an obstacle to democracy. That is mainly due to the rise of radical political Islamic movements that have their own interpretation of Islam and Koran, according to which democracy is *'haram'* (means forbidden in Arabic). Therefore, they are likely to stand against it and seek to establish the Caliphate.

But the Arab Spring comes in a time when uprisings swept some Muslim countries, like Indonesia, Malaysia and Lebanon (a country with majority of Muslims). Indonesia, as the largest Muslim country, successfully overthrew its authoritarian regime late 1990s, after 32 years of Suharto's reign, and Malaysia followed its democratization example. The first wave of the Arab Spring has swept away many regimes. These changes will allow us asking the question, will the Arab Spring revolutions be a starting point to theorize the fourth wave of democratization that started in Indonesia in 1997? Or will the Cedar revolution in Lebanon be the starting point of the fourth wave that is mainly an Arab wave?

The Arab Spring turned out to be an "Arab Winter" with the return of tyrant regimes in many Arab Spring countries, civil war in Yemen, failed states of Libya and Syria, and the rise of ISIS as a transnational peril. With these developments on the ground, would the second wave of the Arab Spring break out soon? We believe that it is just matter of time to see millions of people pouring to the streets again chanting, "People want to overthrow the regime". The same causes and circumstances that ignited and fueled the first wave still exist.

Bibliography

Books and Journals

Acemoglu, Daron. "From Education To Democracy?" *The American Economic Review*. Vol. 95. No. 2 (2005), pp. 44-49.

Almond, Gabriel A. and Verba, Sidney. *The Civic Culture: Political Attitudes and Democracy in Five Nations.* London: Sage, 1989.

Atassi, Mohamed Ali. What People Want." Khoury, Doreen, Abu-Ayyash, Anbara, and Paul, Joachim. (eds.). *Peoples' Power: The Arab World in Revolt.* Berlin: Heinrich Böll stiftung, 2011, pp. 28-34.

Courbage, Youssef and Todd, Emmnuel. *A Convergence of Civilizations: The Transformation of Muslim Societies.* George Holoch. (trans.). New York: Columbia University Press, 2011.

Dewey, John. *Democracy and Education: An Introduction to the Philosophy of Education.* New York: Macmillan Company, 1916.

Elbadawi, Ibarahim and Makdessi, Samir. "Introduction." Elbadawi, Ibarahim and Makdessi, Samir. (eds.). *Democracy in the Arab World: Explaining the Deficit.* New York: Routledge, 2011.

Fahimi, Farzaneh Roudi, and Kent, Mary Mederios. "Challenges and Opportunities: The Population of Middle East and North Africa." *Population Bulletin*. Vol. 62. No. 2 (2007), pp. 2-18.

Glaeser, Edward, Ponzetto, Giacomo, and Shleifer, Andrei. "Why Does Democracy Need Education?" *Journal of Economic Growth*. Vol. 12. No. 2 (2007), pp. 77-99.

Hart, Daniel, Atkins, Robert, Markey, Patrick, and Youniss, James. "Youth Bulges in Communities: The Effect of Age Structure on Adolescent Civic Knowledge and Civic Participation." *Psychological Science*. Vol. 15. No. 9 (2004), pp. 591-597.

Huntington Samuel. *The Third Wave: Democratization in the Late 20th Century*. Paperback, 1993.

Inkeles, Alex. "Making Modern Men, On the Causes and Consequences of Industrial Change in Six Developing Countries." *American Journal of Sociology*. Vol. 75. No. 2 (1969), pp. 208-225.

Lijphart, Arend. "Comparative Politics and the Comparative Method." *The American Political Science Review*. Vol. 65. No. 3 (September 1971), pp. 682-693.

Lipset, Seymour Martin. "Some Social Requisites of Democracy: Economic Development and Political Legitimacy." *The American Political Review*. Vol. 53. No. 1 (1959), pp. 69-105.

Lynch, Marc. *The Arab Uprising: The Unfinished Revolutions of the New Middle East*. New York: Public Affairs, 2012.

Mansfield Peter. *A History of The Middle East*. Revised and Updated by Nicolas Pelham. Penguin Books. 2013.

Pehrson, Rander and Davis, Justine. *Germany and The Revolution of 1848-1849*. New York: Peter Lang, 1999.

Pennock, James Roland. *Democratic Political Theory*. Princeton: Princeton University Press, August 1979.

Ramadan, Tarik. *L'Islam et le Réveil Arabe*. Paris: Presses du Châtelet, 2011.

Urdal, Henrik. "The Demographics of Political Violence: Youth Bulges, Security, and Conflicts." Brainard, Lael and Chollet, Derek. (eds.). *Too Poor for Peace? Global Poverty, Conflict, and Security in the 21st Century*. Washington D.C.: Brookings Institution, 2007, pp. 90-100.

Youssef M. Tarek, "Development, Growth and Policy Reform in the Middle East and North Africa Since 1950," *Journal of Economic Perspectives*, Vol. 18, No. 3 (Summer 2004). p. 91-116.

Ziadeh, Radwan. "The Syrian Revolution: The Role of the 'Emerging Leaders." Zunes Stephen et al. *Revolution and Political Transformation in the Middle East.* Washington: The Middle East Institute, 2011, pp. 43-45.

Zunes, Stephan. "The Power of Strategic nonviolent Action in Arab Revolution." Zunes, Stephen et al. *Revolution And Political Transformation in the Middle East.* Washington: The Middle East Institute, 2011, pp. 9-13.

Internet Sources and Databases

Agbor Julius, Taiwo Olumide and Smith Jessica, "Sub-Saharan Africa's Youth Bulge: A Demographic Dividend or Disaster?" http://www.brookings.edu/~/media/research/files/reports/2012/1/priorities%20foresight%20africa/01_youth_bulge_agbor_taiwo_smith. (Search date:December 19, 2012)

Al-Rashdan, Abdul Fatah Ali. "Higher Education in the Arab World: Hopes and Challenges." http://www.isn.ethz.ch/isn/Digita

Library/ Publications/Detail/?ots591=0c54e3b3-1e9c-be1e-2c24-a6a8c7060233&lng=en&id=103115. (Search date: April 11, 2011)

Al-Tamimi, Jumana. "Women fuel Arab revolts." http://gulfnews.com/news/region region/women-fuel-arab-revolts-1.772905. (Search date: September 15, 2012)

Andoni, Lamis. "Bahrain: Historical Struggle." http://www.aljazeera.com/indepth/opinion/2011/08/20118301473301296.html. (Search date: June 7, 2012)

Bishara, Marwan. "In the Arab world, the West's interests trump its values." http://aljazeera.com/indepth/opinion/2012/02/20122141 21210448673.html. (Search date: November 14, 2012)

Cabras, Antonello. "The Implications of The Youth bulge in MENA Populations." http://www.nato-pa.int/Default.asp?SHORTCUT =2342. (Search date: November 12, 2012)

"Challenges to Human Security in the Arab Countries." http://www.arabhhdr.org/publications/other/ahdr/ahdr2009e.p df. (Search date: November 15, 2012)

Chamberlain, Kenneth. "Timeline: Revolt in the Middle East and North Africa." htt p://www.nationaljournal.com/timeline-revolt-in-the-middle-east-and-north-africa 2011 0128. (Search date: November 7, 2012)

Cheterian Vicken, "The Arab Revolt: Roots and Perspectives," http://www.isn.ethz.ch/isn/Digital-Library/Publications/Detail/?ots591=0c54e3b3-1e9c-be1e2c2a6a8c7060233&lng=en&id=127332. (Search date: September 11, 2012)

Cincota, Richard P. "Half a Change: Youth Bulges and Transition to Liberal Democracy." http://wisloncenterorg/sites/default/files/ECSPReport13_Cincotta.pdf. (Search date: September 12, 2012)

Coll, Steve. "The Second Tunisian Revolution: A New Model of Change for a New Generation." http://www.usmep.us/usmep/wp-content/uploads/2011-18-USMEPolicy-Brief1.pdf. (Search date: September 17, 2012)

"Creating Opportunities for Future Generations." http://www.arabhdr.org/publicationshdr.org/publications/other/ahdr/ahdr2002e.pdf. (Search date: November 21, 2012)

"Education for All: Literacy for Life." http://www.uis.unesco.org/Library/Documents /gmr06-en.pdf. (Search date" July 25, 2011)

"Education Indicators: Technical guidelines." http://www.uis.unesco.org/Library/Documents/eiguide09-en.pdf. (Search date" July 22, 2011)

El-Hawat, Ali. "Funding Higher Education in The Arab States: Thoughts and Reflections on the Topic." http://unescore-clic.org/node/114. (Search date: October 11, 2012)

Fergany, Nader. "Arab Higher Education and Development: An Overview." http://www.ties-project.eu/sites/uni4inno.eu/files/Arab%20HE%20deve lopment.pdf. (Search date: July 22, 2011)

"Gender-Sensitive Education Statistics And Indicators: A Practical Guide." http://www.uis.unesco.org/Education/Documents/unesco-gender-sensitive-edstats-indicators.pdf. (Search date: March 11, 2012)

Gladwell, Malcolm. "Small Change: Why the Revolution Will Not be Tweeted." http://www.newyorker.com/reporting/2010/10/04/101004fa_fact_gladwell?currentPage=all.(Search date: November 12, 2012)

Hamzawy, Amr. "Understanding Arab Political Reality: One Lens Is Not Enough." http://www.carnegieendowment.org/files/PO15.hamzawy.FINAL.pdf. (Search date: September 17, 2012)

"How Many Shia Are There In The World?" http://www.islamicweb.com/beliefs/cults/shia_population.htm. (Search date: September 22, 2012)

Karolak Magdalena Maria, "Civil Society and Web 2.0 Technology: A Study of Social Media in The Kingdom of Bahrain," http://www.arabmediasociety.com/articles/downloads/20110531112812_Karolak.pdf. (Search date: December 21, 2012)

"Kingdom of Bahrain: General Profile." http://www.unesco.org/fileadmin/MULTIMEDIA/INSTITUTES/UIL/confintea/pdf/National_Reports/Arab%20States/Bahrain.pdf. (Search date: September 13, 2012)

Lynch, Marc. "Obama's Arab Spring?" http://mideast.foreignpolicy.com/posts/2011/01/06/obamas_arab_spring. (Search date: November 7, 2012)

Malcomson, Scott. "Bahrain: The Widening Gulf." http://6thfloor.blogsnytimes.com/2011/03/16/bahrain-the-widening-gulf. (Search date: July 5, 2012)

Marlar, Jenny. "Global Unemployment at 8% in 2011: Youth are Three Times More Likely Than Older Adults to be Unemployed," http://www.gallup.com/poll/153884/global-unemployment-2011.aspx. (Search date: December 21, 2012)

Mirkin, Barry. "Population Levels: Trends and Policies in the Arab Region: Challeng- -es and Opportunities." http://www.arab-hdr.org/publications/others/ahdrps/paper01-en.pdf. (Search date: November 12, 2012)

Morris, Steve. "Using Digital and Social Media During A Crisis Tackling The Proliferation of New Communications Channels." http://www.portland-communications.com/using-digital-and-social-media-during-crisis. (Search date: September 17, 2012)

Satti Osman Mohamed, Nour Samia. "Assessment of The State of Women and Gender Gap in Sudan." http://www.arab-api.org/conf_0310/p27.pdf. (Search date: July 23, 2012)

Satti Osman Mohamed, Nour Samia. "Education, Training And Skill Development Policies In Sudan: Macroand Micro Overview." http://www.merit.unu.edu/publicatio ns/wppdf/2011/wp2011-032.pdf. (Search date: February 13, 2012)

Schwartz, Stephanie. "Youth and the Arab Spring." http://www.usip.org/publications/youth-and-the-arab-spring. (Search date: November 11, 2012)

Shank, Michael. "How the Arab Spring Sprung From a Nonviolent Source." http://huf fingtonpst.com/michael-shank/arab-spring-source_b_974836.html. (Search date: April 11, 2012)

Stepanova, Ekaterina. "The Role of Information Communication Technologies in the Arab Spring: Implications Beyond The

Region." http://www.gwu.edu/~ieresgwu/asse ts/docs/ponars/pepm_159.pdf. (Search date: September 27, 2012)

"The Road Not Traveled Education Reform in the Middle East and North Africa." http://siteresources.worldbank.org/INTMENA/Resources/EDU_Flagship_Full_ENG.pdf. (Search date: September 11, 2011)

"Towards Achieving the Millennium Development Goals: Progress of Work (2004-2007)." http://www.undp.org.bh/Files/2008MDGPROREP/IntroductionBHR-MDG-PROREP.pdf. (Search date: July 23, 2012)

"Unlocking the Employment Potential in the Middle East and North Africa Toward a New Social Contract." http://web.worldbank.org/WBSITE/EXTERNAL/COUNTRIES/MENAEXT/0,,content MDK:20260961~pagePK:146736~piPK:146830~theSitePK:256299,00.html. (Search date: September 11, 2011)

Watins, Kevin. "Education Failures Fan The Flames In The Arab World." www.efareport.wordpress.com/2011/02/23/education-failures-fan-the-flames-in-the-arab-world. (Search date: September 12, 2012)

Williamson, Andy. "Social Media and the New Arab Spring." http://www.hansardsociety.org.uk/blogs/edemocracy/archive/

2011/04/19/social-media-and-the-new-arabsprin g.aspx. (Search date: November 15, 2012)

"Women And The Arab Awakening Now is The Time." http://www.economist.com/node/21532256. (Search date: August 11, 2012)

Wrigly, Patrick. "Youth Bulges in The Middle East and North Africa: Risk or Assets?" http://cmimarseille.org/_src/SELM4_WB FastBrief74.pdf. (Search date: January 12, 2012)

Yazbeck, Natacha. "In Arab Revolts, Women Emerge As Driving Force." http://www.thejakartaglobe.com/international/in-arab-revolts-women-emerge-as-driving-force/42 7281. (Search date: September 12, 2012)

Young, Krysten. "Democratization in the Middle East and North Africa: Challenges Explanations and Suggestions for the Future." http://web3.unt.edu/honors/eaglefather/wp-content/2011/08/Young-Krysten-081711-Final.pdf. (Search date: November 13, 2012)

Zakaria, Fareed. "The Politics Of Rage: Why Do They Hate Us?" http://www.thedailybeast.com/newsweek/2001/10/14/the-politics-of-rage-why-do-they-hate-us.html. (Search date: Nov 15, 2012)